THE RADICAL EMOTIONAL REGULATION AND SELF-LOVE WORKBOOK FOR ADULTS

DAILY CBT EXERCISES AND PRACTICAL STRATEGIES TO BREAK FREE FROM NEGATIVE EMOTIONS AND WELCOME HAPPINESS

S. S. LEIGH

CONTENTS

THE RADICAL SELF-LOVE WORKBOOK FOR ADULTS
A Mindfulness Guide With Daily CBT Exercises to Break Free From Self-Criticism, Doubt And Social Anxiety (Boost Confidence, Self-Esteem, Happiness)

S. S. Leigh

EMOTIONAL REGULATION SKILLS TO OVERCOME TOXIC THINKING AND BEHAVIOR

Get Out of Your Head and Calm Your Thoughts With Practical Strategies and Exercises; Stop Anger, Anxiety, Jealousy, and Insecurity

S. S. Leigh

Special Bonus!

Want This Bonus Book for FREE?

Get __FREE__, unlimited access to it and all my new books by joining the Fan Base!

SCAN W/ YOUR CAMERA TO JOIN!

THE RADICAL SELF-LOVE WORKBOOK FOR ADULTS

A MINDFULNESS GUIDE WITH DAILY CBT EXERCISES TO BREAK FREE FROM SELF-CRITICISM, DOUBT AND SOCIAL ANXIETY (BOOST CONFIDENCE, SELF-ESTEEM, HAPPINESS)

S. S. LEIGH

"You yourself, as much as anybody in the entire universe, deserve your love and affection." —Buddha

INTRODUCTION

Around 10 years ago, I had a serious problem – I wanted others to love me, but I didn't love myself! I was frustrated, desperate, and depressed. I could not understand why I was so unfortunate that every relationship I got into would fall apart. It wasn't hard to tell that all my romantic relationships followed the same pattern. They would start on a high note, and then, as soon as I would become genuinely invested in the relationship, the other person would pull away.

I would desperately try holding onto that person, but in my heart, I always knew – it was over! For years, I cried myself to sleep every night. I felt overwhelmed by these questions – "Why me?" "Why am I the only person in the world who can't stay in a relationship?" "Am I ever going to get married?" "Why does love elude me every single time?"

I was so deeply trapped inside my victim mindset that I couldn't recognize the role I was playing in the destruction of my relationships. Besides, it wasn't just my romantic relationships that were dysfunctional. Pretty much all my relationships were in shambles.

I felt lonely and dejected every single day. Simply staying alive felt like the hardest thing I had to do every single day. There were so many days when merely getting out of bed seemed like a massive accomplishment. I dreaded mornings because very morning when the sun would come up, I'd realize that the option of escaping into dreamland was no longer available to me. I had to face reality – the reality that I was lonely and miserable. Nothing in my life was going the way I would like it to.

I felt like a loser – a total failure. It had become impossible for me to hold on to a job or to a relationship. Even my family didn't want to be around me. I had no real friends. I often turned to food and television for comfort. My 'reality' was so excruciatingly painful that I was able to find comfort only in the world of make-believe.

One day I had a major altercation with my boss at work. It made me really upset. I felt certain that I was going to lose my job. To escape the pain and misery I was feeling, I headed to a bar right after the workday ended. Over there, I got so drunk that to this day I have no clear recollection of exactly what happened on that evening. All I can remember is I got in my car to go back home and then a giant tree showed up out of nowhere. I felt terrified that the tree was going to devour me. After that, I blacked out completely.

When I came back to my senses, I was in a hospital bed with all kinds of tubes and pipes attached to my body. At first, I had no idea where I was or how I got there in the first place. Very soon I learned that I had experienced a head-on collision with a giant tree while driving back home. My car had been completely damaged in the accident. It was a miracle that I was still alive!

The next few days were very hard. Every inch of my body was hurting. I wasn't able to eat food or drink water properly. It was in those darkest hours of my life that I had a profound realization. I didn't want to die – I wanted to live. It's just that I wanted a better life than what I had had until that point.

At that moment, I also realized that I had been taking so much for granted. When it was excruciatingly painful to swallow food or drink water, I suddenly realized that even the ability to swallow food and drink water is a huge blessing. It is so tragic that we don't understand the value of what we have until it is taken away from us. In those moments, I learned that nothing in life should ever be taken for granted.

That day I made a promise to myself – I was going to improve my life! I committed to doing whatever it takes to turn my dream life into a reality. I decided that I was either going to succeed in creating my dream life or I'd die trying. Even the latter felt like a far better proposition than the idea of continuing to waste my life writhing in self-pity and indulging in self-destructive behavior. I wanted to be genuinely happy, and, this time, I had decided I wasn't going to sit around waiting for happiness to come find me. I was going to proactively do whatever it takes to become the happiest, most joyful person I can ever be.

Once I got out of the hospital, my passionate quest for self-improvement began. I signed up for a gym membership so I could take excellent care of my body. Next, I added a simple five-minute meditation to my morning routine. I became steadfastly committed to my newly adopted self-care regime.

From that point on, self-improvement became my obsession and passion. I studied any valuable information I could find on the subject - be it through courses, books, mentors, or coaches. At that stage of my life, I was so desperate to feel better that I was willing to try anything and everything that could possibly help me on any level.

Slowly, things started improving. I began feeling better about myself. Most importantly, I began to understand who I was, what I wanted, and who I wanted to be in this life. Eventually, I was also able to find another job that was better aligned with my core values and talents.

I still had days when I would struggle to get out of bed. Sometimes, I would even slip back into full-blown depression and dejection. But I was also learning to be more resilient. I realized that it didn't matter how many times I fell down. What matters is how quickly I can get back up on my feet again.

FALL IN LOVE WITH *yourself*

As I made progress on my self-improvement journey, the amount of time I needed to get myself back up kept reducing. Even now, there are days when I fall down but I have trained myself to get back up immediately. If you'll follow everything that I will be teaching you in this book, then you'll be able to do the same as well.

Going back to my story, I started spending a lot of time at a local bookstore that specializes in self-help and spirituality-related books. I would spend hours in the bookshop browsing through self-improvement books. One day a book caught my eye. I felt powerfully drawn towards it. It was a book on CBT (Cognitive Behavioral Techniques). I flipped through the first few pages and I immediately knew I had to buy it.

This is how I got introduced to the world of CBT. Since then, I have read countless books on this subject. My problem with most CBT books is that they are often too academic and full of hard-to-understand jargons. As a reader, I would have liked a book that was simple and easy to understand. I wanted practical guidance on how to immediately start applying everything I was learning to my own life.

I am writing this book now for you because this is the book I wish I had when I was looking for guidance. I had to learn things the hard way through a lot of trial and error. With this book, I want to simplify the process for you so that you can apply CBT to your life a lot more easily and, thereby, get results much faster.

Quite early on in my self-improvement journey, I realized that my relationships with others were never going to work unless I improved the most important relationship in my life – my relationship with myself! By using CBT techniques and methods, I was able to take practical action to change my life, my emotions, and my mind.

I hope this book will guide you to love yourself. I am sharing my best techniques, tools, and methods with you here. I will only ever share with you what has worked for me personally. I hope this book will help you create a happier and more fulfilling life for yourself.

No matter what you are going through right now, you have the power and the ability to emerge victorious. I believe in you!

DECLARATION OF COMMITMENT

The extent to which you are going to benefit from this book depends entirely upon the level of commitment you have towards absorbing all the information I am sharing here and doing all the exercises. To get results, you have to go all in. If you are ready, then write your name and sign the statement of declaration. If you feel you aren't ready yet, then come back again after some time once you feel you are ready to go all in.

__I would highly recommend that you use this book every single day until you have studied all the information and completed all the exercises. Even if all you can manage is a few paragraphs a day, it is better than sporadically using the workbook. Consistency is the master key to success. You can go at your own pace – just make sure that you are studying each chapter thoroughly and completing all exercises as best as you can.__

Write your declaration of commitment here and seal it with your signature.

THIS IS MY BINDING COMMITMENT TO:

_____

_____

_____

_____

_____

Signature

1

DO YOU LOVE YOURSELF?

"Owning our story and loving ourselves through that process is the bravest thing that we'll ever do."

— BRENÉ BROWN

As human beings, we are wired to seek love. The problem is that we are taught from a young age to seek it outside of ourselves instead of focusing on cultivating it within ourselves. No matter how much someone loves you or cares for you, they can never give you what you don't have for yourself. I had to learn this truth the hard way. I desperately kept trying to get others to love me. The irony was the harder I tried, the faster my relationships fell apart.

The problem with expecting someone to give you what you are not giving to yourself is that they could be doing the best that they are capable of, but it may not exactly be what you want. We all desire love, but how each one of us defines and experiences love is often unique to us. We have different needs, and our unique personality traits determine the distinctive way in which we like to give and receive love.

By default, we try to give others what we ourselves want to receive. Hence, the way we give and express love to another person is determined by how we like to receive love ourselves. This is why someone may be doing the very best that they are capable of but it may not feel fulfilling to us. This is simply because they are expressing their love in a language we do not resonate with.

Also, even if you are with someone who gives and receives love in the same way as you do, it doesn't guarantee that you'll feel fulfilled by it. Let me explain this with the help of an analogy. I was sitting by the river bank one day. For fun, I dug up a small hole in the sand and started filling it with water that I brought from the river. As soon as I poured water into the hole I had dug, the water would disappear. At first, I was puzzled. Eventually, I realized the receptacle that I had created in the sand was simply not capable of containing the water inside it.

In the same way, we cannot fully receive and accept someone else's love unless we make ourselves a perfect receptacle for receiving it. Someone can pour all their love and affection onto you, but it may leave you feeling empty and depleted simply because you have not developed the capacity to absorb what they are giving you. You must first build a perfect receptacle by practicing radical self-love.

Self-love is the beginning of every kind of love. I am sure you have already heard the saying that no one can pour from an empty cup. Indeed, you cannot give to someone else what you don't have for yourself. I don't think it is an exaggeration to say that we can truly love another human being without being in love with ourselves first. Trying to pour from an empty cup causes a buildup of resentment and grudges.

It is an unfortunate truth that women are taught to be extremely self-sacrificing from a very young age. Little girls are often conditioned to believe that their needs don't matter. They are taught to put their own needs behind everyone else's. I am not saying that we shouldn't make sacrifices for the greater good of the family unit or for society at large, but if you'll keep doing it all the time, then that is certainly going to deplete you.

I meet so many mothers who feel their family takes them for granted. These wonderful women wake up every morning at the crack of dawn and spend all day catering to the needs of their families. They take no time to look after themselves. By night, they are bone-tired and ready to crash into bed. The problem is that they want to fill everyone else's cup without filling their own first.

Of course, this can be just as true for men as it is for women. In our society, men have their own unique struggles. For instance, they are taught to suppress their emotions and never express their authentic feelings. Men are also expected to make different types of sacrifices for the greater good of family and society. It can lead to resentment and a deep sense of unhappiness if they aren't filling their own cup first.

WHY YOU MUST FILL YOUR OWN CUP FIRST

The biggest problem with not filling your own cup first is that it compels you to have unrealistic expectations of others. You start depending upon other people for your happiness, but there is no one in this world who can fulfill such an expectation (absolutely, no one!). Also, if you don't have unconditional love for yourself, then you just can't have it for another human being either. No matter what you say or believe, it is simply not possible.

The question of someone taking you for granted arises only when you are expecting something in return for what you are giving. Besides, if you are doing things with the expectation of receiving something back, can we really call it unconditional love?

Whenever I am about to do something for someone, I always ask myself one question: "Would I do it even if I received nothing in return – not even an acknowledgment?" If the answer is "yes," then I know it is the right thing for me to do. But if the answer is no, then it would be better for me to not do it.

Saying no is not easy. We want to please others – that isn't necessarily a bad thing. The problem is if you are trying to please someone else by putting yourself in a very uncomfortable position, then you are inevitably going to come out of that experience feeling depleted and resentful. You have to think about yourself first. If you are bargaining your own happiness to please someone else, it's just not worthwhile.

Fill up your own cup first!

You should never do something for someone else expecting something in return. Give to others unconditionally, or don't do it at all. I am not talking about being self-sacrificing here. All I am saying is that you have no control over someone else's behavior no matter how close you are to them. If you are looking for something (even if it is only a desire for acknowledgment or praise), then you are setting yourself up for disappointment.

There is absolutely no guarantee that you are going to receive what you want. If you'll verbally demand that the other person give you what you are looking for, then the chances are even lower that you'll receive it. On the other hand, when you do things for others because that's just what you want, the act itself becomes a reward. If you receive an acknowledgment, praise, or any other reward in return, you're able to appreciate what you are receiving better.

Always remember that you can never have a wonderful relationship with another human being without first having a beautiful relationship with yourself. To genuinely love someone else, you have to be in love with yourself first. Hence, self-love is the foremost kind of love. If you feel you don't have enough love in your life right now, then it is time you need to start filling your own cup first.

WHAT DOES IT MEAN TO LOVE YOURSELF?

The older I get, the more I realize that love is a verb and not a noun. Unlike what the movies suggest, love doesn't just happen. It has to be cultivated through action and intention. You have to consistently and constantly do things that help you feel loved and cared for.

When couples say they have fallen out of love after having spent a decade or so together, I genuinely feel sorry for them. Pop culture makes people believe that the heady feeling of infatuation is love. This is why people enter relationships expecting it to be all roses and sunshine with no effort required on their part. Would you expect a garden to remain prim and perfect if you never tended to it? How can you expect to have a great relationship with yourself or with others if you aren't intentionally putting in the effort for it.

Relationships make life beautiful, but they also require constant tending to. You have to invest in your relationships if you want them to be amazing and fulfilling. I hope by now, you understand that the most important relationship in your life is the one you have with yourself. You teach others how to treat you by the example of how you are treating yourself.

If you constantly keep bashing yourself and then you wonder why your partner never accepts you for who you are, it is time to look within. Even if you are the only person who is ever going to hear the negative self-talk inside your head, at the energetic level, it impacts every single relationship you are ever going to have. It's not an exaggeration to say that your relationships with others are a reflection of your relationship with yourself.

When I was addicted to finding flaws in my physical appearance, I used to end up with men who were also hyper-critical of my looks. Once I changed my perception of myself and I accepted myself as the amazing person that I am, other people started affirming my awesomeness as well.

Now that we have established that love is a verb defined by action and not just a feeling, let us explore some of the ways in which we can practice self-love. As you read through the next subsections, think about how many of these things you are practicing now. If you aren't already practicing any of these, then think about how you can incorporate these ideas into your life.

At the end of this chapter, I'll also share a quiz with you where you can check your score to see where you stand on the self-love spectrum. It will help you better understand your starting point. When you know what you are starting out with, it becomes easier to know how you need to move forward to achieve your goal.

Talking to and About Yourself with Love

From now on, I want you to become very conscious of your self-talk. What is that voice in your head telling you right now? Does this voice encourage you to achieve your goals or does it keep pulling you down? Does this voice appreciate you or is it constantly criticizing you? Keep in mind the fact that thought is the precursor of all action. How you are talking to yourself determines what kind of action you are taking in your life.

If you are constantly criticizing yourself, then it is likely that you are also not doing much to squash your limiting beliefs. You cannot achieve anything worthwhile in life without first believing that you are worthy and deserving of what you desire.

It is also very important that you start becoming conscious of how you talk about yourself to others. Are you always putting yourself down in front of others or do you talk about yourself with confidence and pride? Now, I am not talking about being cocky. Authentic self-confidence comes from a place of self-love and humility.

When you truly love who you are, you don't feel the need to try and prove yourself to others. You know you are enough and your opinion of yourself is all that truly matters. People who come across as cocky and full of themselves do not really believe in themselves. Their cockiness stems from deep insecurity lying underneath the veneer of over-confidence.

From now on, start becoming more observant and conscious of what you truly think about yourself. The self-talk inside your head and the conversations you are having with others about yourself will give you all the data you need to understand how you see yourself.

Another important thing to observe is how you respond to compliments. Do you feel comfortable and uneasy when someone pays a compliment or do you accept compliments graciously? If someone gives you a compliment and you counteract it by putting yourself down, then that means you don't really love yourself. Worse still, it is likely that you don't feel deserving of praise and appreciation.

Feeling Worthy and Deserving

Do you feel worthy and deserving of the good things you already have in your life and of the things you desire? Most of the time we don't get what we want because deep down, we don't feel worthy of it. This can be true for your dream career, your dream marriage, or just about everything else in life.

I used to think there was nothing I wanted more badly than a relationship. For as long back as I can remember, I wanted to get married and have a family of my own. As I shared earlier, I had no issues attracting wonderful potential partners into my life. Things would start off on a high note, but my world would come crashing down equally fast. Yes, I can blame those people and say things like, "There are no good people left in this world." But this isn't the truth.

This world has all kinds of people in it. We don't attract what we want. We attract who we are. When we don't feel worthy and deserving of what we want, we stand in our own way of getting what we want. In my case, I managed to attract the type of potential partner I wanted into my life. Things would start out well and then I would subconsciously start sabotaging the connection.

Deep inside, I felt unworthy of what I was receiving. At the surface level, I thought I was amazing but deep inside I believed I didn't deserve to be loved. I would have a hard time accepting the fact that a wonderful desirable person would want to be with me. My subconscious mind would start looking for signs that the person was cheating on me or worse still, I'll start waiting for them to call things off with me. Eventually, whatever I'd be expecting would turn into a reality –all thanks to my self-fulfilling prophecies!

It is very easy to point the finger at others or blame the world for our problems. But when we dare to look deep inside, it becomes obvious that all the problems in the outside world manifest from our own subconscious mind. The outside world serves as a perfect mirror to our inner world. If you can't convince your subconscious mind that you are worthy and deserving of what you desire, then what you want is going to continue eluding you in the external world.

Again, how you talk to yourself and about yourself will give you a better understanding of how you perceive your self-worth. Trust me, you are perfectly worthy and deserving of all that you desire. You just have to start believing it! It's okay if right now you have no idea how to make it happen.

Just the fact that you have picked this book up and you are reading it right now demonstrates that you are ready for a change. I truly commend you for this. Most people say they want to change their life, but they never take any action to make it happen. You are already doing well because you are truly willing to make the desired changes. Stay committed – I promise you won't be the same person by the end of this book, provided you'd do all the exercises and put into action everything I am sharing with you.

Knowing, Understanding, and Prioritizing Your Own Needs

Most people are so out of touch with themselves that they don't even know what their needs are. If you are one of them, then it is time to start focusing on developing greater self-awareness. To live a fulfilling life, you have to know what your physical, mental, emotional, and spiritual needs are.

Every day, you must intentionally cater to your body, mind, and soul. This means prioritizing your "me-time." If you aren't already scheduling any "me-time" into your day, then it is high time that you start doing it.

What it looks like in practice differs from person to person, but the essence of scheduled "me time" is that you must spend time looking after your body, mind, and soul. This could mean engaging in some form of physical exercise, meditation, breathwork, reading, practicing affirmations, etc.

You don't have to do all of these things every day. You can pick a few that you resonate with and add them to your daily routine. Just make sure that you are doing at least one activity every day for all three aspects of your being: mind, body, and soul. Stay committed to doing things that energize you and help you recharge your batteries.

You can also schedule different activities for different days if you are someone who thrives on variety. As I said earlier, every single day, you must schedule the time to look after your body, mind, and soul. This shouldn't feel like work. It should feel refreshing and something that you look forward to doing every day. The idea may seem overwhelming right now if you already have an over-packed schedule, but you must get started.

Also, if you have so much on your plate that you are constantly feeling overwhelmed, then it is time to start prioritizing your tasks more efficiently. Start delegating what you can to others. For instance, ask your children to help lay the table so that you can serve dinner faster.

At work, don't shy away from asking for help from a colleague who can help you complete your tasks better. Most of the time we don't receive the help we want because we never ask for it. Trust me, your loved ones want to lighten your burden. But for that, you must tell them exactly how they can help you out.

If you think you have to do everything yourself because no one can do everything as well as you can, then that's a different kind of issue. You have to let go of your perfectionism if you want to be happy in life. So many people overload their platter by taking up more responsibilities than they are realistically able to handle.

Remembering to practice Pareto's Principle really helps me in this case. It is so true that only 20% of the things create 80% of the results (Wikipedia, n.d.). Busyness doesn't indicate productivity. You have to become really good at identifying those 20% things that contribute to 80% of your results. Once you start focusing on doing more high-impact activities and fewer low-impact activities that don't contribute much towards your goals, it gets easier to delegate tasks to others.

There are only 24 hours in a day. You just can't afford to keep running around in circles like a hamster on a wheel. It is absolutely crucial that you take the time to look after yourself. You deserve your own love and care. You should spend at least 1-2 hours every day taking care of yourself physically, mentally, emotionally, and spiritually. You are worth it!

SELF-LOVE QUIZ

I have designed this quiz to help you understand how committed you are to self-love. Even if you get a low score, I would urge you to not feel bad about it. This quiz is not a measure of your self-worth but of the degree of self-love you have. It is okay if you don't have enough self-love right now.

This book is about radical unconditional self-love which means you are willing to accept and love yourself in spite of all your perceived and real imperfections. So if currently you don't have a lot of self-love in your heart, it is okay - you must accept yourself exactly the way you are right now.

A quiz like this helps you gain perspective. You'd know which areas you are weakest in and, hence, you can work on strengthening yourself in those areas. The questions where you scored the lowest will show you your areas of weakness. Make a special note of these and then dedicatedly work on improving yourself in these areas.

I would strongly recommend that you take this quiz twice - once at the beginning of your journey and again after completing chapter eight. Make note of your initial score. It would be fascinating to observe how far you'd have come by the end of the eighth chapter.

For each question, give yourself a score on a scale of 0-4. This is what each number indicates: 0 = strongly disagree, 1 = disagree, 2 = neutral, 3 = agree, 4 = strongly agree. Use the scoring guide at the end of this quiz to understand your results.

1. When you look in the mirror, you feel good about your body. _____
2. You forgive yourself for the mistakes you have made. _____
3. You enjoy your own company when no one is around. _____
4. You like taking care of yourself. _____

5. You regularly make time for self-care. _____
6. You are proud of who you are. _____
7. You don't take other people's criticism of you personally. _____
8. You believe in yourself. _____
9. You trust that you can achieve any goal you set your mind upon. _____
10. You feel you are a lovable person. _____
11. You rarely ever feel the blues. _____
12. You love your life. _____
13. You trust your judgment and decisions. _____
14. You are committed to personal development. _____
15. You are always looking for ways to be better. _____
16. You know how to love yourself while also aspiring to be an even better version of yourself. _____
17. You talk positively about yourself to others. _____
18. Your self-talk with yourself is positive, uplifting, and encouraging. _____
19. You feel comfortable saying 'no' to things you don't want to do. _____
20. You never allow anyone to trample your boundaries. _____
21. You are very good at delegating the less important tasks to others. _____
22. You regularly do things that help you feel renewed and refreshed. _____
23. You love and accept yourself unconditionally with all your perfections and imperfections. _____

24. You know that your presence adds value to other people's lives. ____
25. You know that you are a valuable person. ____
26. You always know what's best for you. ____
27. You are kind to yourself. ____
28. You know your voice and your opinions are important. ____
29. You are assertive when it comes to establishing and maintaining your boundaries. ____
30. You feel comfortable being yourself around others. ____

Your Total Score: _____

SCORING GUIDE

Use this guide to understand your results.

100-120 – You really do love yourself! This is wonderful. This book will help you develop even greater self-love. Love, after all, is a verb. The more positive actions you take to cultivate self-love, the better your life is going to be. You are on the right path.

You are already doing well. The questions where you scored slightly low will indicate to you those areas where you can improve even further. Stay committed to self-love. Always remember that no matter how far you have come, there is always another level you can reach!

70-100 – You do love yourself to a certain extent but there are areas where improvement is needed. This is wonderful news because if you are doing well in certain areas, then it shouldn't be too hard to improve in other areas. The questions where you scored slightly low will indicate to you those areas that you should focus on in this journey of self-improvement.

You are going to benefit greatly from this book as we are going to discuss many practical ideas that you can use to cultivate deeper self-love. If you'll do everything I am going to share with you, then you'll definitely have a different score by the time you finish this workbook.

>70 – You are in the right place. It is okay if you are struggling with self-love. The fact that you have picked this book up shows how committed you are to changing your life. You just need the right guidance, and that's something this book is going to provide you with. I would urge you to remain committed to this journey. Do all the exercises in this book with due diligence. Take the time to mull over the wisdom encapsulated in each chapter.

Think about how you can immediately put into practice what you are learning. Whenever you start feeling engulfed by the clouds of self-doubt, reaffirm to yourself, "I am committed to self-love. I am worthy and deserving of love and acceptance." Practice this affirmation as frequently as you need to and also use it to fill moments of silence when your mind beings wandering aimlessly here and there. Stay on this journey, and you'll definitely be a different person by the end of chapter eight!

2

RADICAL SELF-LOVE BEGINS WITH RADICAL SELF-ACCEPTANCE

"Self-love has very little to do with how you feel about your outer self. It's about accepting all of yourself."

— TYRA BANKS

R adical self-love begins with radical self-acceptance. You cannot love yourself in the truest sense of the word without first accepting yourself completely. Indeed, I am talking about accepting yourself exactly the way you are – with all your positive and negative qualities.

You cannot put off practicing self-love until another day when you'll be a better version of yourself. You have to love who you are right now. There is nothing worse than giving yourself a shifting goal post putting off self-love for another place and time. I did it to myself for years so I know exactly how that feels. I stopped aiming for perfection only once I realized a profound truth about human life. No matter how far you come in life, there is always another level to aspire to. Perfection is an illusion that can never be attained – it is much better to strive for excellence instead.

Life can never be fulfilling without self-love. If you think you can start focusing on self-love once you have achieved your goals or when you are a better person than who you are today, it's never going to happen. This is akin to an over-weight person saying they will start exercising once they have lost 50 pounds. It just doesn't happen!

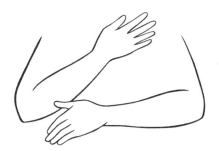

Your struggles with self-love are closely related to your lack of self-acceptance. The irony is that we want others to accept us for who we are when we repeatedly fail to accept ourselves for who we are. Again, I want to emphasize the fact that no one can give you what you are not giving to yourself. If you want others to accept you fully for who you are, you must commit to self-acceptance first.

In my past relationships, I used to get very upset and disappointed because my partners wouldn't accept me for who I am. They would constantly try to change me and put me down by being hypercritical of me. Blaming them for being unkind and inconsiderate was the easy thing to do, but when I sat down to really look within, I realized that they were showing me a reflection of my own relationship with myself. How could I expect someone else to accept me when I was not accepting myself for who I was?

Also, because I was so broken inside and desperate for love, I was attracting and feeling attracted to people who didn't love themselves. Since they were lacking in self-love, they were also struggling with self-acceptance. As I said earlier, no one can accept another human being unless they learn to fully accept their own self first.

There is really nothing worse than two broken people trying to have a relationship together. It is doomed to be dysfunctional because both parties are trying to extract out of the other person something they are not capable of giving to themselves. I didn't accept myself so my partners didn't accept me for who I was. While I was busy complaining about their lack of acceptance towards me, I failed to realize another profound truth: I wasn't able to accept them for who they were either!

Think about it – if I was being truly accepting of them would I complain and crib so much about how they were making me feel? If you want to have a peaceful and fulfilling relationship with another human being, then you have to accept them exactly the way they are. No matter how hard it is for you to accept this fact, the truth is you cannot change another human being. The harder you try, the worse your relationship is going to get because no one wants to feel forced to change for someone else's sake. If you are currently guilty of this, then stop, please!

Now, I am not suggesting that you should be a doormat in your relationship with others and accept however badly they may choose to treat you. Of course, not! Authentic self-love is all about having strong boundaries. You have to say 'no' and walk away when your needs are not being met in a relationship or when a relationship is draining you in some way.

Real self-love is the ability to be comfortable with yourself and perfectly happy in your own company. When you are content with yourself, you stop getting into relationships out of the fear of being alone. You love yourself too much for it. If you aren't there yet, then don't worry, you will get there. Trust me, the fact that you are reading this book and doing all the exercises tells me, you are committed to self-improvement.

Success is all about showing up. No matter how far out of reach the goal may seem, for now, you'll definitely achieve it provided you remain committed to the path and keep doing the work. Moving forward, complete and unconditional self-acceptance should be your motto.

WHERE DOES LACK OF SELF-ACCEPTANCE COME FROM

Our early life experiences have a powerful impact on who we become as adults. If our parents didn't make us feel unconditionally accepted for who we were as children, it is inevitable that we'll struggle with self-love in our adult life. I am not saying this so that you can place the blame on your parents and not take full responsibility for your lack of self-love and self-acceptance. That would be extremely disempowering!

No matter what happened in your life, you have to take full responsibility for who you are right now and for everything that you have or don't have in your life. Taking responsibility doesn't mean you have to blame yourself for all the unfortunate things that have happened in your life. It simply means you are ready to claim your power to rise above the past. Who you want to be and how you want to live your life is entirely in your own hands. You are the only one who has the power to choose your present and your future. You can either be a victim or the master of your destiny – it is your choice entirely!

It took me a long time to get out of the victim mindset. I spent a lot of time blaming my parents and my early life experiences for the things that weren't going well for me. Nothing good came out of it. I just kept wallowing in the cesspool of self-pity. Eventually, I had one very profound realization. I was operating from the perspective that my parents are supposed to be perfect because they are my parents. Society plants this idea in our minds that parents are supposed to have all the answers. Just because they have given birth to children, they must have all of life figured out. In reality, this is hardly ever the case.

Accept yourself

When I started thinking of my parents as fellow human beings on a similar journey as mine, I stopped having such expectations. I realized that they did the best that they were capable of based on the knowledge and understanding they had. In their flawed ways, they tried to do the best for me. I also realized that their inability to accept me was rooted in their lack of self-acceptance. In fact, this is true for everyone. It takes a tremendous amount of self-awareness and an intense commitment to self-improvement to foster that kind of radical self-acceptance. Most people fail miserably at it so we can't blame them for not giving us what they aren't able to give to themselves.

Besides, not everyone is interested in self-improvement the way you and I are. The fact that I am writing this book for you and you are reading it shows that we both have an intense desire to be better versions of ourselves. I am sharing what I have learned in my own journey of self-evolution and you are learning from it so that you can create similar results for yourself. It is important to keep in mind that not everyone thinks like this. Most people want to remain confined to their comfort zone. It is not our responsibility or even our right to judge their journey no matter how close we are to them.

My parents didn't know any better when they made me feel less than accepted for who I was. Chances are that's how their parents treated them as well. It is also likely that's how their parents' parents treated their parents. The cycle of misery gets passed on from one generation to another until someone intentionally decides to break it. Since you are reading this book, you can become that person for your family.

You have empowered yourself with the understanding that to truly accept another human being, you have to accept yourself first. Hence, you have also developed the ability to give to others what you may not have received from them. Keep your cup so full with radical self-acceptance and self-love that you can easily share your abundance with others.

Something miraculous happens once we begin practicing radical self-acceptance and self-love. The people who were hypercritical of us either start distancing themselves from us or they may even disappear from our lives. We also start attracting new people into our lives who accept and love us unconditionally.

It is also possible that our existing relationships may undergo a complete transformation. Others may suddenly become a lot more accepting and loving towards you. It happens because the external world is truly a mirror of our inner world. Unlike what most people believe, real transformation is always an inside-out process. You cannot change anything in your life without first transforming your own self in some way.

FORGIVENESS IS ESSENTIAL FOR ACCEPTANCE

You must forgive your parents for the things they didn't do right – they just didn't know any better. But first, you must forgive yourself for the things you yourself didn't do right. It is okay to be imperfect. It is okay to not get everything right all the time. It is okay to make mistakes. Your past doesn't have to be a life sentence – learn from it and let it go.

Human beings are not supposed to be perfect. You must let go of this idea that there is something wrong with you because you have flaws and shortcomings. Trust me, there isn't a single person on this planet right now who isn't imperfect in some way. No matter how perfect someone may look, every single person on this planet is deeply flawed.

Owning your flaws and shortcomings is extremely empowering. Magic happens once you stop criticizing yourself for not being perfect. When you stop demanding perfection from your own self, you also stop expecting it from others.

Forgive yourself for all your mistakes - learn from them but don't let them hold you hostage. When you forgive yourself, it gets easier to forgive others. Remember, you can never give to someone else what you don't have for yourself. To forgive your parents and everyone else in your life, you must start by forgiving yourself first.

EXERCISE

Set an hour or two aside and write a letter of forgiveness to yourself. Address this letter to yourself as if you were writing the letter to your best friend. In other words, be just as kind and thoughtful towards yourself as you would be towards your best friend. While writing the letter, think of what you would say to your best friend who has been feeling guilty about past mistakes. You deserve to hear such kind and encouraging words just as much as your best friend does.

Writing this forgiveness letter is often an extremely cathartic process. Once you shift your perspective and start seeing yourself as your best friend, you suddenly realize just how hard you have been on yourself all this time. You deserve to be treated better. The journey to greater self-love begins with forgiveness.

Forgive yourself for all your past mistakes – you did things the way you did because you simply didn't know any better. Now, you have evolved into a finer version of yourself. Moving forward, you'll do everything better. Learn from the past but let go of it. Take your time to write this letter as thoroughly as possible. You can also set aside an entire day for doing it. Write down every single mistake and fully express all the negative emotions you have been holding on to.

I would recommend that you do this exercise in a peaceful place. Turn your phone off and let your family know you are going to need some time by yourself. Request them to not disturb you unless it was an emergency. No matter how busy you are and how many responsibilities you have to fulfill, you deserve some time by yourself. Ask for help from others so that they can take charge of your duties while you take this time to work on yourself.

You can also play some soft music in the background and light a few candles to help create a relaxing atmosphere. Allow yourself to feel all the emotions that come up during this process. Don't try to suppress them. Let them rise fully – own them, accept them, embrace them. No emotion is bad.

Every emotion is there to help us experience the full spectrum of human life. We cannot embrace happiness without also embracing sadness. We cannot embrace joy without also embracing pain. We are taught from an early age that certain emotions are bad. We begin suppressing these emotions. That's how emotional and psychological issues take root in our consciousness.

Once we start fully accepting all our emotions, the negative ones stop having so much power over us. Always remember: what you resist, persists. The best way to make yourself feel an emotion at its full intensity is by striving to not feel it at all. By trying to resist something, you give your power to it.

Instead, embrace all the emotions that are arising in your consciousness. Allow yourself to revisit and relive the past. IT IS OKAY THAT YOU WERE NOT PERFECT AND IT IS OKAY THAT YOU ARE NOT PERFECT NOW. Give up this burden of perfection. If you have learned from the past and you are striving to be better today, then you are doing well.

After writing the letter, you can burn it and release the ashes into a flowing water body. If you don't have access to a flowing water body, then you can also flush the ashes. If you don't want to burn the letter, then you can also make small pieces of it and bury it in the earth. The point is to release and let go of all that you have held onto for so long. After completing the release ritual, you'll experience an immediate shift. You'll feel lighter – as if a load has been lifted of your shoulders.

SELF-ACCEPTANCE QUIZ

After completing the letter-writing exercise, come back here and take this self-acceptance quiz. If you haven't done the letter-writing exercise yet, then I would advise you to go back and do that first. You would definitely experience a massive shift, and when you get back to taking this quiz, the results would be a lot more encouraging.

Again, the point of this quiz is not to make you feel about where you are in life right now. The purpose of this quiz is to help you better understand where you currently are on the self-acceptance spectrum. Knowledge is power. By having a thorough understanding of where you are right now, you can steer your efforts in the right direction. The areas where you score the lowest are the areas that need your maximum attention.

No matter what your score turns out to be, accept and embrace your results. You are perfect the way you are no matter what the scores say. Self-acceptance isn't about embracing a mythical perfect version of yourself. It is all about fully owning and embracing yourself exactly the way you are.

Lastly, keep in mind that self-love and self-acceptance aren't traits we are born with. They are skills anyone can develop with intentional practice. The fact that you are reading this book and doing these exercises tells me you are committed to developing these skills. Stay committed – you'll definitely get the results!

For each question, give yourself a score on a scale of 0-4. This is what each number indicates: 0 = strongly disagree, 1 = disagree, 2 = neutral, 3 = agree, 4 = strongly agree. Use the scoring guide at the end of this quiz to understand your results.

1. I know who I am. _____
2. I am perfectly lovable exactly the way I am. _____
3. I allow others to love me. _____
4. It is easy for me to be kind to myself. _____
5. I am very good at taking care of myself. _____
6. I enjoy looking after myself. _____
7. I truly believe that it is okay to be imperfect. _____

8. I forgive myself for my mistakes. _____

9. I understand that I am imperfect just like everyone else in this world. _____

10. My imperfections make me unique and charming. _____

11. I am a valuable human being. _____

12. It is easy for me to be honest with myself. _____

13. Most of the time, I take full responsibility for my life and my own actions. _____

14. I don't bash myself for my mistakes. I learn from them and release them quickly. _____

15. I rarely indulge in self-sabotaging behavior (like over-eating, overspending, constantly looking for signs of cheating in a relationship, etc.). _____

16. I trust I can handle anything that comes my way. _____

17. I trust the process of life. _____

18. I am grateful for my past because it has made me who I am today. _____

19. I have no regrets in life. _____

20. I am proud of the life I have lived so far. _____

21. I feel blessed. _____

22. My destiny is in my own hands. _____

23. I know my strengths. _____

24. I know how to use my strengths to create favorable results. _____

25. I know what my weaknesses are. _____

26. I believe I can turn my weaknesses into strengths.
    _____

27. I own myself completely and unconditionally. _____

28. I love all aspects of myself. _____

29. Most of the time, I live in the here and now. _____

30. I am not a prisoner of my past. _____

Your Total Score: _____

SCORING GUIDE

Use this guide to understand your results.

100-120 – You are doing well! Self-acceptance is an art you have mastered to a great extent. Keep practicing self-acceptance and self-love. Growth is a never-ending process. You can always raise yourself to an even higher level of authentic self-love and self-acceptance. Make a note of those places where you scored the lowest. In the next exercise, I will show you how to take your game to a whole different level!

70-100 – You do accept yourself to a certain extent. With practice, you can increase your level of self-acceptance. Go back to your score sheet and observe where you scored the lowest. Make a note of those statements. In the next exercise, I will show you how to convert these negative statements into positive affirmations. Again, self-acceptance and self-love are skills we develop and not traits we are born with. The more you practice, the better you are going to get it.

>**70** – I know you are struggling with self-acceptance. IT IS OKAY! You don't have to bash yourself for your scores on this quiz. This score is not a reflection of your worth as a human being. You are a valuable and wonderful human being who deserves the very best. Accept yourself for who you are right now. By doing just this, your life will begin to change for the better. Self-acceptance means you are ready and willing to accept every single aspect of your being. This includes the fact that you struggle with self-acceptance. You'll soon realize that it all becomes less of a struggle once you start embracing everything instead of resisting it.

EXERCISE – AFFIRMATIONS

Positive affirmations are a perfect tool for counteracting negative self-talk. I want you to go back to the previous exercise and pick all the statements where you received a low score. For instance, let us assume that you scored really low on this statement: "I believe I can turn my weaknesses into strengths."

Now, turn this into a positive affirmation by writing it in the present tense as if it were already true for you. This is what it would look like, "I have mastered the art of turning my weaknesses into strengths."

Here's another example for the same statement: "I feel blessed." You can turn this into an affirmation like this: "I love how blessed I feel every single day of my life."

Be sure to write your affirmations in the present tense as if what you are affirming is already an established truth in your life. Moving forward, whenever you start feeling negative, go back to these affirmations and read them out aloud or in your mind. Also, get in the habit of reading them every morning and evening at least seven times. Ideally, you'd want to read them a minimum 21 times every morning and evening.

The best time for practicing affirmations is early in the morning immediately after you get out of bed and at night right before you fall asleep. At these two times of the day, the doorways of the subconscious mind are wide open. Since your subconscious mind creates your reality, you can transform your life only by transfiguring your subconscious blueprint. Affirmations are a perfect tool for this purpose.

The more frequently you practice an affirmation, the more strongly it becomes rooted in your subconscious mind. Hence, the more strongly it impacts your life. I want to give you another powerful affirmation that you can add to your daily routine. Chant it as frequently as you can. Here it is:

"I love myself wholly, completely, and unconditionally. I accept myself wholly, completely, and unconditionally. I am perfect exactly the way I am. I am worthy and deserving of all that is best and wonderful."

Chant this affirmation as frequently as possible. Also, add it to your morning and evening routine. For more life-transforming affirmations, you can check out my *I am Capable of Anything* series where I have shared unique affirmations that can be practiced three times a day.

3

APPRECIATE YOURSELF

"When you undervalue what you do, the world will undervalue who you are."

— OPRAH WINFREY

When was the last time you patted yourself on the back and said, "Well done!" If you are like most people, then most likely, you don't remember when you did this, or worse still, you have perhaps never done it at all.

If you find it hard to appreciate yourself, then I don't blame you at all. It isn't the norm in society. From an early age, we are encouraged to seek approval and appreciation from others. We are taught that to be "good" we have to do exactly what pleases our parents, teachers, and other authority figures. Hence, it is not surprising that our sense of self-worth becomes tied to the acceptance and approval of others.

LOVE YOURSELF

The problem is that our parents, teachers, and other authority figures are also flawed human beings. Not everything we learned from them consciously or subconsciously is good for us or supports our highest good. As adults, we must do a lot of unlearning if we want to be genuinely happy and live up to our fullest potential.

Seeking acceptance and approval from others compels you to shift your locus of control outside of yourself. Since you cannot control how others see or treat you, you start feeling like a victim of circumstances. Self-acceptance and self-appreciation help you maintain an internal locus of control.

You aren't relying on others to give you what you need. Instead, you learn to give yourself exactly what you need. Once you learn to fulfill your own needs, you become a formidable force of nature. Self-love makes you indestructible. No one can harm a person who is rooted in deep unconditional self-love.

COME TO TERMS WITH YOUR INNER CRITIC

Have you ever seen a baby indulge in self-loathing? I am sure your answer is going to be a resounding "No." Isn't it interesting that we have all been that baby at some point completely in love with ourselves? Yet by the time we grew up, the voice of the inner critic became extremely strong and overpowering.

This inner critic tells you "You are not capable" "You are not worthy" "You don't deserve this" and a million other things that disempower you. It is very hard to silence this inner critic because it seems to yell at you every step of the way. Every time you start making the effort to move beyond the past and create positive changes in your life, it pulls you back.

As a result, you remain stuck in a vicious cycle of feeling unworthy and undeserving. The first step towards conquering and silencing the inner critic involves becoming aware that this voice isn't yours. You internalized this voice based on the criticism and comments you heard from the authority figures in your life while growing up.

Once you start recognizing the fact that this voice isn't yours, it becomes easier to start distancing yourself from it. Whatever this voice is telling you isn't your own truth, but instead, it is someone else's opinion of you. Opinions, as we all know, are biased and flawed.

You don't have to live the rest of your life inside the prison of someone else's opinion. As a child, you didn't have much power over what was told to you. But as an adult, you can enforce strong boundaries and show others how to treat you. Most of all, you have the power to free yourself from the prison of the past. The people in your life didn't know any better but now you can choose to not be affected by their opinions and biases.

What you were told growing up wasn't the fact of your life or of who you are – it was a projection of someone else's reality. Others will say you are incapable of something when, in reality, they believe they are the ones who are incapable of it.

The same applies to all negative ideas and beliefs you were imparted as a child. It is a reflection of someone else's limited worldview. You don't have to accept it. This is why I always say that self-awareness is the first and the most important step in the journey of personal transformation. By being self-aware, you can start distancing yourself from the inner critic that sabotages your growth. That nagging voice inside your head isn't your own voice, and it is certainly not spouting facts at you. It is someone else's voice that has become internalized in your subconscious mind. To progress in life, you must get rid of it.

The best part is that the subconscious mind is programmable. Just like how you can erase old data and write new data on your computer, you can do the same with the subconscious mind. Your conscious mind is that part of your consciousness which remains actively aware of what you are thinking. However, this part of the mind is like the tip of an iceberg – it is very limited in capacity and has only so much influence over your life.

The subconscious mind is that part of your consciousness that almost entirely determines and influences your reality. It is a massive data bank where all your beliefs, ideas, and memories are stored. The interesting thing is that even the things that you think you have forgotten about are never really forgotten by the subconscious mind.

You may think you have eliminated a negative experience from your memory by not thinking about it, but the subconscious never forgets anything. It remembers everything until you go back and rewrite what has become imprinted. For that, you need to consciously use tools like meditation, affirmations, incantations, breathwork, etc. In this book, we'll be using many of these tools to erase negative programming from your subconscious mind.

I am sharing all this with you to help you come to terms with your past. It is important to understand that if you had an overly critical parent growing up, their harshness towards you was a projection of their lack of self-love. Their criticism of you was an extension of their lack of acceptance towards their own self.

As an adult, you may have distanced yourself from that hypercritical parent, and you consciously try to not remember all the painful things they said to you. But the real problem is that their harsh words have become internalized in your subconscious mind. You aren't vigilant of it like you are of your parent in the external world because at a very deep level you have begun to identify that nagging voice inside your mind as your own.

This is also the reason why you may say you want something at the conscious level but your actions and your beliefs don't match that reality. For instance, as I shared earlier, I really thought there was nothing I wanted more badly than a relationship. But every time I got involved with someone, I found ways to sabotage that relationship. I would start hunting for signs of infidelity or for them to leave me until that expectation would become my reality.

What you say or think at the level of the conscious mind has very little value unless you learn to bring your subconscious mind in alignment with it. After all, your thoughts, behavior, and actions are determined by your subconscious mind. This can be done only by intentionally fostering and practicing deep self-awareness.

EXERCISE

Take some time to reflect on what that inner critic is telling you right now. Note down everything it is saying in the space provided below. If you start running short of space, use a notebook or diary to record all your thoughts and emotions.

Moving forward I want you to carry a notebook with you everywhere you go. You can also use a digital diary if you don't want to carry a physical notebook with you. Whenever you start hearing the voice of the inner critic, pull out this diary and start writing everything it is telling you. By simply writing things down, you'll kickstart the process of disassociating from this voice. This practice will also help you practice deeper self-awareness.

At the end of the week, go through everything you have written down. You'll be amazed to notice that before you wrote things down it seemed as if there were a million thoughts in your head. When you look at them in a written format, you realize there are only a handful of thoughts that your mind keeps repeating over and over again. Because of the frequency with which the same or similar thoughts occur, you feel overwhelmed. You feel there are too many thoughts on your mind, but in reality, thoughts are often repeated in patterns.

Once you have identified your thought patterns, you can create your own positive affirmations that counteract the negative thought patterns. Go back to the previous chapter and read the exercise on affirmation creation and practice, if you need to. Moving forward, whenever negative thoughts start pestering you again, replace them with positive affirmations. Repeat these affirmations as frequently as possible. Over time, your mind will begin to accept them as your new reality, but you must persist in your efforts if you want to get results.

TAKE PRIDE IN YOUR ACCOMPLISHMENTS

For most of us while we were growing up nothing we ever did felt good enough. We were told that we need to do better no matter how good our grades turned out or how hard we worked. Our accomplishments were hardly ever celebrated, but our failures or shortcomings were always harshly criticized.

Unfortunately, we end up carrying this attitude into our adult life constantly belittling and being dismissive of our own accomplishments while holding on too tightly to all our real and perceived failures.

From now on, I want you to shift your perspective. Instead of focusing on your failures start celebrating your accomplishments. Of course, you should learn from setbacks and failures, but never allow them to hold you back. You don't have to be a prisoner of your past for the rest of your life. The gate is wide open – you can choose to walk out of this life sentence that so many of us give to ourselves in ignorance.

People often erroneously think that criticism and constant chiding help in achieving goals. Just imagine a beautiful baby in front of you. Every time this baby started walking in wobbly steps and fell down, you'd start scolding the baby harshly. What will happen to that baby? Won't it be utterly cruel to do that? Maybe that baby would even start believing that he was simply not capable of walking and would give up altogether.

But you have a heart – you'll never do this to a baby. My question is why are you doing this to yourself? Why do you expect yourself to do everything perfectly when you are learning something new? Why do you have to treat yourself so harshly? I am sure that if the baby was in front of you right now attempting to take his first steps forward, you'll cheer on the baby. You have to start doing the same for yourself. Start appreciating yourself for the efforts you are putting in, even if you don't get the desired results straight away.

"I would praise you, but
your value is beyond words."

Reward is a much better teacher than punishment. Once you start celebrating your accomplishments, you'll also automatically manifest more reasons to celebrate. Your ability to create results is closely tied to your self-image and your beliefs about yourself. You have to train yourself to see the best in yourself.

You are worthy of your own appreciation and encouragement. Don't let anyone tell you otherwise. You are an incredible human being who deserves the very best. You just have to start treating yourself like you would treat a beautiful baby who was learning to walk. Cheer on yourself, and celebrate all your wins – both big and small.

EXERCISE

In the space below, write down at least 10 major accomplishments you have had that you are proud of. It doesn't necessarily have to be something that is deemed a major achievement by society at large. If it was something significant for you, then it is worth acknowledging and celebrating! For instance, getting back in shape, recovering from a major setback, or anything else that felt like a significant achievement to you should be included in this list.

No achievement is ever too small to be acknowledged and celebrated. When you were feeling low and emotionally distressed, maybe your greatest achievement was simply getting out of bed and getting dressed for the day. It is worth acknowledging and celebrating such an achievement as well.

Get in the habit of recognizing and celebrating all your accomplishments. The more frequently you do this, the more feathers you'll add to your cap!

_____

_____

_____

_____

_____

_____

REWARD YOURSELF GENEROUSLY

If it is important to do loving and caring things for others, then it is all the more important to do those things for yourself. As I said earlier, reward is a much better teacher than punishment. We are all very good at punishing ourselves. Unfortunately, rewarding ourselves isn't something that we think about so much. Just imagine – when was the last time you gave yourself a gift or some kind of reward for your achievements?

More often than not, the answer I receive is "Never!" I am sure if I asked you about the last time you scolded yourself or punished yourself in some way, it won't be that hard to recall that instance. It's alright, though! No one teaches us these things growing up. You are learning something new – it's okay if you don't have a lot of experience doing it so far. Through practice, you can master any habit.

You must appreciate yourself for the commitment you have made to change your life for the better. You are reading this book because you are open to the idea of practicing radical self-love and self-acceptance. Simply being open to this possibility is a significant achievement in its own right.

From now on, I want you to reward yourself regularly for everything you are doing well. Something incredible will happen once you start doing this. You'll be amazed to realize how many things you are already doing well. It's just that you have been so focused on the negative that it seemed like the list of things you weren't doing right was far longer than the list of things you are doing right.

This is generally the case for most people. Once you start writing down all your accomplishments regularly, you start observing that most of the time you are doing well. A shift in perspective is often a lot more important than an immediate change of circumstances. The latter comes a lot more easily once the former is taken care of.

Moving forward, I want you to not just recognize and acknowledge your accomplishments but also celebrate them. Every time you do something that requires you to move outside of your comfort zone or that feels like an important step in the right direction, I want you to reward yourself.

This reward should be something that you really enjoy or cherish having. For instance, a massage, or a favorite meal, and if it is within your budget, then maybe you can also purchase that item you have had on your wishlist for a long time now.

By rewarding yourself for all the good things you are doing, you train yourself to do more of those things that are worth celebrating. Punishment works in the same way. By chiding and punishing yourself for the things you are not doing right, you actually train yourself to do more of those undesirable things. Hence, choose wisely!

EXERCISE

Go back to the previous section where you wrote down your accomplishments. Next to each accomplishment, write down a reward you are going to give yourself. In the next few weeks, let yourself enjoy these rewards.

From now on, get in the habit of acknowledging your successes. Keep a diary handy for noting down all your big and small achievements. Every time you note down an accomplishment, be sure to reward yourself for it. Rewards can be both big and small.

Ideally, it should be proportionate to the size of your accomplishment. For instance, the reward for going to the gym every day for 7 days can be allowing yourself to have a healthy dessert once a week. When you accomplish something big, give yourself a massive reward for it!

I would suggest that you create a list of everything you enjoy doing in a separate notebook, and then, pick something from there to add to your accomplishment journal every time you hit a goalpost.

For starters, write down 20 things here that you enjoy doing the most. You can pick items from this list to add next to your accomplishments in the previous section. You deserve these rewards!

REALIZE THAT YOU ARE NOT THE ONLY ONE WHO IS IMPERFECT

We judge ourselves way too harshly by comparing ourselves with others. We look at the accomplishments of others and compare our weaknesses with their strengths. It's a skewed and unfair comparison that can only cause unhappiness and dissatisfaction.

You must realize that every human being on this planet is imperfect. It may seem like some people have everything figured out, but there really isn't a single human being on this planet who isn't struggling with something or the other. Our strengths and weaknesses are distinct to us. Hence, the nature of our struggles is also different. But I can assure you of one thing – no one is perfect!

Besides, there are certain things that every single human being struggles with. For instance, laziness is one of those things that we all have a propensity for. Of course, the definition of laziness can differ from person to person, but more often than not, we all feel we aren't living up to our full potential. There is something really freeing about having this realization. Once you realize that your struggles aren't something exclusive to you, it becomes easier to accept that there is nothing wrong with you.

Perfectly Imperfect

You can be kinder and more compassionate to yourself when you understand that a lot of the things you struggle with are part and parcel of the human experience. Every human being has to face their inner demons in order to rise to their full potential. Instead of chiding yourself for where you are falling short, keep your focus on encouraging yourself where you are thriving. If you can get in the habit of doing this, then, eventually, you'll master the art of turning your weaknesses into strengths.

EXERCISE

Research the life of someone you admire. If it is a famous person, then try to read their interviews, books, podcasts, or any other material you can find. Delve deep into understanding what they have struggled with and how they overcame their challenges. It is easy to look at the veneer of success and allow yourself to be bewitched by it. You must understand that they got where they are by overcoming hardships and fighting their inner demons.

If this is a person you know in real life, then you can spend some time with them. Ask them introspective questions to learn about their struggles and how they got to where they are.

In the space below, you can write down some of the things this individual has struggled with and a summary of how they overcame it. This will help you realize that they are not that different from you. If they can do it, then so can you!

_____

_____

_____

_____

_____

_____

_____

_____

_____

_____

_____

_____

_____

RECEIVE APPRECIATION GRACIOUSLY

We are taught to give generously, but most of us never learn how to receive graciously. Giving and receiving are two sides of the same coin. If you are only giving and never allowing yourself to receive, then you'll never experience authentic fulfillment. To balance the scale, you must open yourself up to receive more. This gives the people in your life a chance to express their love and care to you.

If you are someone who never accepts help, it is time to make some changes. You don't have to do everything by yourself – it is okay to receive. In fact, receiving graciously can be a deeply enriching experience for both the giver and the receiver. By rejecting the gift someone else wants to give you, you are depriving them of a chance to express their love and care to you.

I want you to start becoming comfortable with receiving the gifts that others want to give you from their heart – both material and energetic. So the next time someone pays you a compliment, don't counteract it by putting yourself down. Instead, just say "thank you." If someone is sincerely paying you a compliment, then that means they are acknowledging and honoring the beauty of your soul.

Counteracting it by putting yourself down is akin to throwing a beautifully wrapped present back at the giver. Would you do it to someone if it was an actual present they handed over to you? Compliments and sincere appreciation are beautifully wrapped gifts. Hold them close to your heart and respond with a simple "thank you" from now on.

Also, be open to receiving material gifts and help of any kind that another person wants to provide you with. If they are doing it from their heart, then it is again a beautifully wrapped present that you wouldn't want to throw back at them.

EXERCISE

For practice, ask a loved one to compliment you today. Visualize that you are receiving a present from them – allow yourself to receive it fully. All you need to say is a simple "thank you" along with a beautiful smile on your face. You must let yourself feel worthy of what you are receiving.

From now on, if someone pays you a compliment, always reply with a simple "thank you." It would help to visualize that they are handing you a beautifully wrapped present – accept it and hold it close to your heart. Never throw it back to them by counteracting it.

4

SPEND TIME WITH YOURSELF

"Spending time alone in your own company reinforces your self-worth and is often the number-one way to replenish your resilience reserves."

— SAM OWEN

We live in a society where distraction is encouraged and spending time alone in quiet reflection is frowned upon. Thanks to the modern world, we have an overabundance of tools to distract ourselves with. If you'll only observe how most people live their lives, you'll realize that they are constantly jumping from one tool of distraction to another.

In fact, the vast majority of modern parents hand over a mobile phone to their children instead of playing with them or getting them engaged in more meaningful activities. The point I am trying to make here is that we live in a society where spending time by yourself isn't considered a priority. To a large extent, solitude and silence are frowned upon.

However, what the masses tend to do is hardly ever the healthy or the right thing. If you look at the lives of the most successful people in the world, you'll realize that they greatly value solitude and quietness. I was reading a book by successful businessman and author John C. Maxwell. The book is titled *How Successful People Think*.

The entire book is dedicated to building the right kind of mindset and cultivating the type of thinking that is most conducive to success. Maxwell emphasizes the importance of spending time alone in peaceful solitude every day. According to him, this is absolutely critical for cultivating your ability to think independently and effectively (Maxwell, 2009).

If you want to be successful in life, then you have to dedicate some time every day to build a stronger relationship with yourself. Always remember that the most important relationship you are ever going to have is with yourself. Hence, this relationship must be prioritized above all else.

Besides, every other relationship you have in life is always going to be a magnified reflection of this one relationship. If you want to improve your relationships with others, then you have to first improve your relationship with yourself. You can never have a healthy relationship with another human being without first having a healthy and wholesome relationship with yourself.

DON'T RUN AWAY FROM YOUR THOUGHTS

Why do you think it is so tempting to spend hours in front of the television? Why is alcohol abuse so rampant in society? Why do we get sucked into the rabbit hole of social media when we go online to check our social media feed for just five minutes?

It is because all these things feel good in the moment. The problem is that they are mere distractions that give us an escape from facing uncomfortable thoughts, feelings, and emotions. They do nothing to help us address the real issue which is often emotional pain.

You can get a temporary escape by indulging in these activities but they also compel you to have a crash immediately after. After watching a movie marathon on Netflix, you feel guilty and disgusted with yourself. When the alcohol begins to wear out, it leaves you with gnawing despair and a pervasive sense of depression.

Also, just because you are consciously not thinking about something doesn't mean that the uncomfortable thoughts and emotions have disappeared. By suppressing thoughts and emotions, you can never get them to disappear. The harder you try to suppress them, the more forcefully they get pushed into the subconscious mind from where they continue to influence your behavior and mindset.

The only way to get rid of uncomfortable thoughts and emotions is by facing them. For this, you have to devote some time every day to spending time in quietude. Set some time aside every day to just sit with yourself. You don't want to resist any thought that comes up during this time. Instead, your goal should be to acknowledge and embrace them fully.

Something truly miraculous begins to happen once you start embracing all your thoughts instead of resisting them. These thoughts almost immediately stop bothering you – they arrive and dissolve in your consciousness like waves in the ocean. They stop pestering you because you are no longer trying to fight them.

Having the witness mindset is very important here. Instead of thinking you are the one who is having these thoughts, start looking at them from a distance from a third-person perspective. Observe how each thought arises in your consciousness of its own accord. Let it appear fully at the forefront of your mind – don't judge it or indulge it in any way. It will disappear quickly without bothering you much.

Unfortunately, we are taught to judge our thoughts. We are conditioned to believe that some thoughts should be encouraged while others have to be fought against. The problem with this ideology is that it goes against a fact of life: whatever we resist, persists.

It is also important to understand that each thought arises from a different part of you. You may think that the 'bad' thoughts you get come from the undesirable parts of you. The label you assign to it is a judgment towards that thought and the aspect of you from which it is arising.

In reality, you don't have any bad or undesirable parts. All parts of you function as a whole to make you the complex and magnificent human being you are. The "bad" "negative" and "pessimistic" thoughts you get arise from those parts of you that want to protect you.

For instance, if you have experienced heartbreak or disappointment in the past, then your mind may seek to caution you to not do anything that can lead to a reoccurrence of the same experience. It is your mind's way of protecting you, but if you judge those thoughts as "negative" and then seek to shun them from your consciousness, they'll start pestering you like the monster under your bed.

Dr. Richard Schwartz has written an excellent book on this subject called *No Bad Parts*. I would highly recommend that you read this book to understand how all the different aspects and parts of you are striving to do the very best for you. You really have no bad or undesirable parts (Schwartz, 2021).

Once you start understanding this idea, it becomes easier to not judge or resist those seemingly "negative" thoughts. Instead, you start listening to what your inner self is trying to tell you, and you become more compassionate towards yourself.

Allow yourself to feel all the emotions that arise in the landscape of your consciousness – each one has its own unique purpose. We cannot function as wholesome and complete human beings without allowing ourselves to experience the full spectrum of the human condition. It includes all thoughts and all emotions arising in our consciousness.

EXERCISE

Set aside 10 minutes every morning and evening to just be quiet and fully present with your thoughts and emotions. Remove all distractions – switch off your phone or put it on airplane mode. Tell your family you are doing something important, and they shouldn't come to you unless it was an absolute emergency.

If possible, try to maintain a dedicated room or a corner in your home where you can do this practice every day. You can also do it by going to a park and spending time alone in nature. Do what works best for you. Just make sure that there are minimal external distractions. Keep your environment as peaceful and quiet as possible.

When uncomfortable feelings, thoughts, and emotions start arising – do not resist them. Instead of judging them visualize them as waves arising and disappearing in the vast sea of your consciousness. Sit with the feeling of discomfort. After a while, it will stop bothering you. Practice being a witness – that's the most powerful technique you can master.

In the space below, write down when and where you'll be doing this practice every day.

PRACTICE JOURNALING

A lot of times, we don't realize or understand what our thoughts are until we begin to write them down. I would encourage you to maintain a separate diary or notebook dedicated solely to journaling. You can use a digital diary or notebook as well.

That being said, I feel writing things the old-fashioned way on pen and paper tends to be a lot more powerful when it comes to journaling. There is a lot of research that shows how writing with a pen and paper engages the brain in a more powerful way than typing (Jones, 2020). But if you absolutely don't want to use a physical journal, then using a digital one is okay. Anything is better than not doing it at all!

You can use journaling any time of the day to clarify your thoughts and ideas. Writing is an extremely powerful practice. It allows you to develop a deeper and clearer perspective on things. Journaling also enables you to feel lighter because when thoughts are confined to your mind, they often feel extremely overwhelming. By writing things down, you realize that it is usually just a handful of thoughts that your mind repeatedly brings up.

Journaling is an excellent tool for finding solutions. If you are confused about something, then writing down all your thoughts related to that subject will help you look at everything from a distance. You will be able to evaluate better what you should be doing to get the desired results.

I would strongly recommend that you do your journaling in a peaceful and quiet environment. Do your best to minimize distractions. This will help you dive deeper into your thoughts and emotions. You can practice journaling every day or whenever you are feeling overwhelmed by your thoughts. You can also do both – journal every day and also whenever you are feeling overwhelmed.

EXERCISE

Set aside a dedicated notebook or diary for journaling. Start using it immediately. You can write whatever comes to your mind in free flow or you can keep it centered around a specific topic where you would like to gain greater clarity.

I would also recommend that you regularly write down the answers to the questions I have shared below. These questions will help you develop immense self-awareness. Self-awareness is the master skill that you need in your arsenal for realizing all your big and small goals.

For now, you can practice by writing the answers to these questions here. Next time, you can copy these questions into your new journal and write the answers there. I would highly recommend doing this practice at least once a month. You'll be amazed by how your answers change as you grow and evolve into a better version of yourself.

Questions to Ask Yourself

What am I avoiding right now?

_____

_____

_____

_____

_____

What am I focusing on right now?

_____

_____

_____

What do I truly need to focus on right now?

What is my highest priority right now?

What is my most important goal right now?

Am I doing things that take me closer to my goals, or am I spending too much time doing things that are taking me away from my goals?

What should I be doing more of?

What should I be doing less of, or should stop doing altogether?

DO SOMETHING CREATIVE

What do you enjoy doing the most? Is there something you have long wanted to do but can't seem to be able to prioritize it? Do you have a hobby that you genuinely love, but you no longer do it, or you don't give it enough time anymore?

It is important to be productive, but it is also crucial to schedule time regularly to nurture your hobbies and interests. Doing so will help you feel refreshed. You'll be able to get back to work with renewed energy. Creative activity performed for its own sake is also a wonderful tool for getting in touch with your core.

Some people think they are just not the creative type. I refuse to believe that. You only need to look at a joyfully playing child to realize that we are all born creative. At some point, you were also a small child – creative and enthusiastic. As you were growing up, maybe the adults around you told you to do more productive things. You heeded that advice, and slowly your creativity started slipping away.

I'm all for being focused and productive but creativity for creativity's sake has its own importance. Pursuing creative activities you enjoy allows you to just "be" and enjoy the moment. It replenishes your soul. Over time, this feeling of creative fulfillment seeps into all areas of life. Hence, you feel a lot more fulfilled with your life in general.

I would recommend that you get in touch with that inner child who was extremely creative at one point. That child is still alive inside you somewhere. Try to recall what it was that you enjoyed doing the most as a child. Maybe it was painting, making DIY crafts, or something else.

Try doing those activities now and also explore related hobbies. If you still can't figure out something you'd like to do, then research hobby classes. You'll get new ideas for what kind of hobby you can adopt. Try out different things, and then pick what you enjoy doing the most. Never feel guilty about investing time, energy, and resources into nurturing your hobby. It will pay off in more ways than you can imagine.

EXERCISE

Create a list of 10 hobbies that you may be interested in. Pick one from the list that you are feeling drawn to the most and start doing it.

_____

_____

_____

_____

I am ready to start pursuing

SET GOALS AND CREATE AN ACTION PLAN TO ACHIEVE THEM

Most people never achieve anything worthwhile in life primarily because they don't know what it is they want to achieve. To know your goals, you have to first know who you are. You have to identify your core values – the things that are most important to you. Real happiness can be experienced only when your core values and your goals are fully aligned.

To keep things simple, focus on just one goal at a time. Ask yourself what it is that you want to achieve this year. It should be something you truly want and are willing to pay the price for. You have to want something so bad that you are willing to do whatever it takes to get it. Again, knowing your core values and having a deep understanding of who you are as a human being is extremely important for setting appropriate goals.

If you aren't sure what your core values are, then it may take you some time to figure them out. Spend time analyzing what it is that you are really good at. Is there something you enjoy doing so much that you lose track of time while doing it? You can also ask your family and friends what they believe are your strengths. Think of those areas of life where others come to take advice from you. Having all this information will help you gain clarity about your core values.

When it comes to goal-setting, create a vision of what you would like your life to ideally look like a year from now, five years from now, and ten years from now. If that sounds like a lot to figure out, then start with just the one-year mark. What would you like to have achieved by the end of another year? Where would you be living? Who will be there in your life? How would you spend your days?

You must give yourself free rein to answer these questions. Right now, it may seem to you that what you want is impossible. Put your critical mind aside – just imagine what you would want if you knew that anything you wished for right now was going to come true. Put it in writing and trust that it is already yours.

Moving forward, research the people who have already achieved what you want to achieve. Try to learn as much about them as possible. What are their habits? How do they spend their time? What kind of people do they associate with? What is their body language like? How do they dress?

Researching the people who have the results that you want will give you the conviction that what you want is possible. If they can have it, then so can you! I can guarantee you that by learning more about them, you'll realize you have the same potential as them. You just need to start believing in yourself more.

You also need to start taking massive action to achieve your goals. Anyone who is sitting at the top didn't get there by a stroke of luck. Results require action. Outstanding results require massive action. Success is not something you stumble upon. It is something you create through hard work and persistent massive action.

Once you have defined and set your goals, I'd urge you to create an action list. It should include all the things you are going to do to achieve your goals. Create a sequence in which you will implement those action steps and then just get started!

Check in with yourself every day to see whether you are moving away from your goals or closer to them. Every single day of your life should be aligned with your goals. At the end of each day, take the time to define what you'd like to achieve the next day and also reflect on how much you have progressed that day. You don't have to spend a lot of time doing this. Even 5 minutes of self-evaluation is better than none.

On the weekend you can spend a little more time analyzing your progress and results. I would also advise you to create an action plan for the coming week. It doesn't have to be as detailed as your daily action list, but you do need to have an idea as to what you'd be doing in the coming week.

EXERCISE

Set some time aside to complete this exercise. Try to do this in a relaxed and calm state, away from all distractions.

Write down three core values that are most important to you.

What is your most important goal for the next year?

Write down at least five action steps you can take to achieve your goal. At least one of these action steps should be something that you can start doing immediately.

SCHEDULE THE TIME TO RELAX AND JUST BE

It is absolutely imperative that you regularly schedule the time to relax and just be. This should be the time that you spend doing nothing or you do only those activities that help you relax. You want this time to be as peaceful and nurturing as possible. For instance, you can spend time in nature or you can create a peaceful environment at home by lighting some candles and playing soft music.

The goal here is to slow down and become fully present in the moment. You can also schedule a massage to help yourself relax deeply. Do whatever feels good to you! Give yourself the freedom to simply enjoy this time by yourself away from all responsibilities, demands, and obligations.

I would strongly recommend that you schedule at least one hour every week to relax deeply. If you feel this is impossible for you, then I would urge you to reassess your life, and how you are allocating your time. Maybe you are trying too hard to do everything on your own. Practicing radical self-love means staying open to receiving help from others. For this, you have to be willing to ask for help – give others the chance to do something for you. Your loved ones really do want to support you – you just need to tell them exactly how they can do it.

A lot of people struggle with delegation because they believe they are the only ones who can perform a task satisfactorily. Nothing good can come out of being such a perfectionist about everything. If someone else can perform a task at least 80% up to the standard you have set for it, then it is worth delegating that task.

You can also hire paid help wherever necessary to reduce your burden. Don't put so much strain on yourself. Do the best you can, but prioritize your well-being above all else.

EXERCISE

Schedule one hour this week to relax and just be. Specify which day and at what time you are going to do it. Be sure to follow through on your commitment.

_____

_____

_____

_____

_____

_____

5

HAVE A VISION FOR YOUR LIFE AND FOR WHO YOU WANT TO BE

"A vision is not just a picture of what could be; it is an appeal to our better selves, a call to become something more."

— ROSABETH MOSS KANTER

In our modern society, almost everyone boasts of being busy. But how many people have a vision for their life and for who they want to be? Some will even say they are too busy to create a vision for themselves. How counterintuitive does that sound? Busyness without a vision is akin to running around in circles like a hamster on a wheel. To get to your destination, you must first sit down and determine exactly where you want to go.

Think about it – do you just get inside your car and start driving without a destination in mind? Obviously not! That would be crazy. Why would you waste your time, energy, and money driving aimlessly? Yet when it comes to their own life most people keep driving helter-skelter without any idea of where they want to go or how they are going to get there.

I think the biggest reason why most people don't have a vision for their life or for who they want to be is because they believe what they want will never happen. As children, we used to genuinely believe anything and everything was possible. Growing up, the adults around us started telling us how this or that wasn't possible.

We were told to dream within our limits and not to spread our wings too far wide lest we may fall. What they accepted as their own truth, they attempted to transmit to you. Their ideas and beliefs about life are not facts but are projections of their own limited worldview onto you.

Now, maybe you are wondering why talk about things like goals and vision in a book about radical self-love. I want to discuss these topics with you because authentic self-love is not about taking a break from your regular life to sometimes do things that nurture your body, mind, and soul. It is about creating a life that you love so much that you do not need to take a break from it at all.

To truly fall in love with yourself and your life, you must develop intense self-awareness. You can't accept yourself completely unless you acknowledge and understand who you are. Similarly, you can't love your life in the truest sense of the word without practicing gratitude for all the blessings you already have while doing the work to get what you want.

Even if you don't believe what you want is possible, isn't it better to die trying to create what you want than to live a life of hopelessness? Besides, when you have a burning desire for something and you are willing to move beyond all your self-imposed limitations to achieve your goals, all the forces of the Universe align to support you.

You are the only person who knows what your dream is and you are the only person who can turn your dream into a reality. You have to first start believing that what you want is possible. If there is just one person in this world who has what you want, then that means it is possible for you as well. Never envy anyone. Instead, look at others for inspiration.

Celebrate all successes – including those of others. Something miraculous begins to happen when you get in the habit of celebrating both your own successes and those of others.

The Universe starts recognizing that you are someone who really likes success. So you start receiving more reasons to revel and celebrate.

THE DIFFERENCE BETWEEN A GOAL AND A VISION

Since we discussed goal setting extensively in the previous chapter, I think it is important to create a clear distinction between a goal and a vision. On one level, it may seem like they are the same, but that's not true.

A goal is a milestone of achievement that you set for yourself within a specific timeline. For instance, it may be something you want to achieve a year down the line, two years down the line, and so on. Vision, on the other hand, is something that encompasses your entire life. It is the larger picture within which everything occurs. Vision is like the vast infinite sky while big and small goals are like planets and stars in that sky.

Your vision encompasses the larger picture of what you want your life to be like while your goals are smaller pillars of achievement that contribute towards materializing it. If you haven't thought about your vision yet, then it is time you do it now. A life without a clear vision is in many ways a life without meaning.

You can set accurate goals for yourself only when you know what your vision for yourself and your life is. Otherwise, you may achieve what you set out to achieve only to realize that it isn't really what you wanted in the first place. If you completed the exercises in the previous chapter, then by now, you would have a clearer idea about your core values. Knowing your core values is essential for crafting an inspiring vision for your life. So if you haven't completed the exercises in the previous chapter, then go back right now and complete them.

YOUR VISION SHOULD BE YOUR OWN

From childhood, we are told who we should want to be – study hard, get a decent job, get married, and have children. Even if you manage to hit all these goalposts, you may still feel deeply unfulfilled. This generic template of what success should be like doesn't make most people happy.

You may or may not want all the items on this list. The biggest thing that is missing from the list is the acknowledgment of your own individual mission, purpose, and vision. We are not taught to think of life in these terms, but that's what is essential for experiencing authentic fulfillment.

We live in a society where consensus and conformity is rewarded from an early age. We are taught to regurgitate premade answers instead of being encouraged to think for ourselves. As adults, we have to do a lot of unlearning if we want to be genuinely happy.

Each one of us is unique and irreplaceable in our own way. You have come into this world to do something that is completely unique to you. You have to identify what YOUR vision for your life is. I am not talking about the vision that family, friends, and society have given you, but the vision you carry deep inside your own heart.

It is time to step into the light and fully own this vision. This is where your power and your potential lie. All dreams can be realized. You don't have to know how your vision will turn into a reality, you just have to fully embrace it. The Universe will pave the way for it to be realized. Of course, you need to do your part as well by taking massive action daily – do the work and leave the rest to the Universe. Life will continue to unfold in magical ways and your vision will continue turning into a reality.

You must take your chances and allow yourself to believe in all possibilities. Whatever you want is within your reach. You just have to be willing to shed the baggage of your limiting beliefs and reach for the sky – quite literally!

EXERCISE

Take the first steps towards creating a vision for who you want to be and the type of life you want to live by answering these questions.

What is it that moves you? (Your vision should fill you with positive emotions and enthusiasm.)

What do you long for?

If you knew that whatever you wanted was going to happen, what would you ask for?

_____

_____

_____

_____

What kind of a person do you have to be to live this dream life?

_____

_____

_____

_____

IDENTIFYING YOUR MISSION AND PURPOSE

Your mission and your purpose are other important pieces of the puzzle that are essential for creating your ideal vision. Your mission summarizes what you are here to do. Your purpose gives you the motivation and the drive to pursue that mission.

For instance, let us say you are a counselor. Your mission can be "to help people explore and embrace their fullest potential." Your purpose can be "to make the world a better place by helping others realize their fullest potential in this life."

Your vision for your life is "to spend every day of life doing something good for others." Your vision for yourself is "to be the kind of person who adds tremendous value to other people's lives."

I hope, by now, it is becoming clear to you what the difference between your mission, purpose, and vision is. Even if it is still not clear to you, there is no need to fuss too much about it. Just write what makes sense to you right now. You can always refine and modify things later on. In fact, as you keep learning, growing, and evolving into a higher version of yourself, you'll feel compelled to redefine all aspects of your life.

It is also possible that you have already evolved to a level where you have great self-awareness about who you are and what you want out of life. In that case, your vision, purpose, and mission statements may remain the same for the rest of your life. Just keep in mind that nothing is set in stone. You can always revisit these things and redefine them to suit who you are at the time or who you want to be.

Most people never give any thought to these things. You are already much further ahead in the game by simply attempting to define your mission, purpose, and vision. You don't have to get everything right immediately, but you definitely need to take the first step right away. The longer you'll put off defining your mission, purpose, and vision, the greater you'll delay living the life of your dreams. Don't be just another one of the masses who are trapped in the limited paradigm that was given to them by others. Let your magnificence shine – your time is NOW!

EXERCISE

Write down your mission, purpose, and vision statements as succinctly as possible. Let it be short and precise – one or two lines at the most. These statements should evoke a strong emotional response in you. Every time you read them, you should feel excited and enthusiastic. If they don't affect you at a deep emotional level, then keep refining them until they do.

It's okay if you can't get to that point right away – write everything down anyway. If you keep working on your statements, eventually you'll reach a point where they begin to feel powerful and inspiring. Simply getting started and consistently taking action are the only real keys to success.

My mission in life is

_____

_____

_____

_____

My purpose in life is

My vision for my life is

My vision for myself is

TURN YOUR VISION INTO A REALITY

Knowing your vision is essential but taking action to turn that vision into a reality is even more important. In the absence of massive action, goals, and vision become mere wishful thinking. Nothing worthwhile can be achieved in life without consistent massive action. I have said this before, and I'll say it again: taking action isn't enough – you need to take massive action! Taking massive action once in a while is also not enough – you have to consistently take massive action.

What does it mean to take massive action? It means you challenge yourself to get more done than most people do in a week, a month, or a year. We try to convince ourselves that we are doing our best but taking a closer look often reveals that we are operating at or below 40% of our intrinsic capacity. Next time, you think you are doing your best or that you have given your all, ask yourself if it is really the truth.

I am absolutely sure your answer will be "No," provided you are being completely honest with yourself. You have infinite potential for growth and excellence. You can always do better than what was your best yesterday. Growth is the one and only constant in the experience of human life. What is not growing and evolving is decaying and dying. If you want to thrive in life, then you have to constantly challenge yourself to do better today than how you were doing things yesterday.

When you are beginning to feel tired or you think you have done enough, challenge yourself to stretch yourself by another 10% to see what you are capable of. Once you achieve that, challenge yourself to stretch by another 10%.

Keep doing it constantly and consistently – you'll be amazed by how much potential you have for growth and excellence.

I am not suggesting that you should push yourself so much that you get burned out. On that note, I feel it is important to define this word properly. This term gets tossed around a lot and almost everyone thinks they are experiencing burnout when in reality they are not even operating at their optimum capacity. I experience burnout only when my heart, mind, and soul are not aligned with what I am trying to accomplish. So if you think you are going through burnout, it is time to really evaluate who you are and what you want out of life.

The distance between your dreams and reality is called action

If you study the lives of the most successful people in the world, you'll realize they all have one thing in common – they love their work! It is extremely difficult to work hard at something you hate doing. You can do it for some time, but encountering burnout is inevitable in that case. Successful people work all the time, but they don't get burned out because they love their work.

I understand that you may not currently be in a position where you can claim to love your work – that's alright! It took me a very long time to figure out who I am and what my purpose in life is. Besides, it's not enough to adopt a profession you love. You also need to make sure that there is a market for it. You need to be able to make money while enjoying working on your passion. So there has to be a demand and a marketplace for what you want to offer.

When you love your work, you'll be more committed to polishing your skills and abilities. Hence, you'll be able to stand out more in your field or niche. The more distinct and irreplaceable you become, the higher you are going to rise in your career.

In other words, taking massive action in a field of work you actually enjoy is much easier than struggling to take massive action doing something you hate. If you haven't figured out what you love doing, then keep exploring. Continue diving deeper into your core values. The better you understand your mission, vision, and purpose, the easier it will be for you to identify a career that suits you.

Having a career doesn't always have to mean working at an office. Maybe your core value is investing in your family. In that case, your vision can be about living a fulfilling family life. You may want to materialize that vision by being a housewife or househusband. That is also totally fine! You have every right to live life on your own terms. There is no one size fits all solution for everyone.

You must do what is best for you even if no one else agrees with you and you to go against the grain. Think about it – a hundred years from now you and everyone else whose opinion you care about won't even be around in this world. Is it really worth giving up on your dreams and your vision to please someone else?

Each one of us has come into this world with a very unique purpose. We must embrace and honor it wholeheartedly. Never hold yourself back from living your best life just because you fear other people's opinions and judgment.

Authentic radical self-love is all about valuing your own opinions and priorities above what others want of you. Besides, every human being is flawed. If others have an opinion about how you should be living your life, it is essentially only a projection of their own biases and limitations.

While you are likely going to have only one mission and one primary purpose in life, you do need to have different visions for each area of your life. You can have one all-encompassing vision for your life and then also have a separate vision for each area of your life. You can set goals for each area of life according to the vision you have for it.

Just make sure that your goals and vision for all areas of life are in alignment with your mission and purpose. In other words, your vision for each area of life should not contradict your mission and purpose. To live a fulfilling life, your purpose and mission need to be fully aligned with the vision you have for the different areas of life.

If you are brand new to all this, then I'll suggest you go slow, taking just one step at a time. Trust me, taking one small step at a time is better than attempting giant leaps in one go. The latter will likely cause you to fall flat, but the former will ensure that you keep making consistent progress toward your goals.

If developing a vision for all areas of your life and having goals associated with each area sounds extremely overwhelming, you can pick just one area that is most important to you right now. It should be an area that you know would have the highest impact on improving the quality of your life. Start working on this area immediately.

As you make progress in this one area, you can start evaluating other areas of your life as well. Over time, you'll be in a better position to develop a vision for and set goals in other areas of your life as well. Success begets greater success. Once you start seeing results in one area of life, you'll automatically feel more motivated to work on improving the other areas of your life.

EXERCISE

Out of the following key areas of life, pick one that is most important to you right now. It should be an area where you know any improvement will have the highest positive impact on the quality of your life right now.

Circle the area of life that you want to work on right now:

Health and Fitness

Career

Finances

Relationships

Intellect

Environment

Spirituality

Charity and Giving

The most important area of life for me right now is _____. For now, I am whole-heartedly going to focus on mastering _____.

Write down your vision for this most important area of life. Make sure that this vision is fully aligned with your mission and life purpose.

_____

_____

_____

_____

_____

_____

Write down all the roadblocks you are going to face as you work on turning this vision into a reality.

_____

_____

_____

_____

_____

_____

Write down the potential solutions for these roadblocks. No matter how insurmountable a problem may seem, there is always a solution for everything. If you can't find the answer right now, then give it time – sit with the problem a little longer. Research how other people have overcome the same issues. Seek out people who have the results you want to create and learn from them.

To be successful, you have to develop a solutions-oriented mindset. Instead of allowing yourself to get emotionally bogged down by problems, you have to put aside all your emotions and focus on logically finding answers and solutions. Emotions enrich our experience of life by allowing us to feel and experience life deeply, but they can also become a roadblock to our success when we give them free rein. You should witness all your emotions like waves arising and dissolving on the ocean floor, but don't let them control you.

From now on, I want you to operate with the mindset that there is a solution for everything. Once you start believing this truth, you'll be amazed by how solutions begin to (almost miraculously) appear. Once you get yourself out of your own way, you can start seeing the possibilities and solutions that have always been around. Yes, they are there even right now! All you have to do is remove the blindfold of your limiting beliefs to see them clearly.

_____

_____

_____

_____

_____

Write down all the steps you are going to take to turn your vision into a reality. Break things down into smaller milestones or goals. Be sure to assign a timeline for achieving each milestone. Ask yourself what you need to achieve next week, next year, in 5 years, in 10 years, and so on.

Focus your energy on what you can achieve immediately within the next week and a month. If you keep moving forward one step at a time, you'll keep getting closer to your dream life. For now, your ultimate goal may seem impossible or improbable, but if you'll consistently keep taking action, then you'll definitely achieve it.

Create your plan right now and start taking action on it from today. When I say today, I mean TODAY! Even if it is a very small step, you've got to start today. That is how you communicate with the Universe. It is a way of saying, you are truly ready to receive what you are asking for, and you are committed to doing whatever it takes to fulfill your desire.

State your commitment to turning your dreams into a reality – you are going to persist no matter what.

I   commit   to

6

CONFRONT YOURSELF AND MASTER YOUR EMOTIONS

"Our deepest fear is not that we are inadequate. Our deepest fear is that we are powerful beyond measure. It is our light, not our darkness that most frightens us."

— MARIANNE WILLIAMSON

If you have completed all the exercises in the previous chapter, then you are likely feeling all fired up. You are ready to start, but there is a voice inside your heart whispering to you all the reasons why you won't succeed. As the euphoria of motivation begins to wear off, this voice becomes louder and more overpowering. You start believing all the nasty things it says: "You can't do this" "Who do you think you are?" "You have nothing of value to offer to the world." The list goes on and on.

Whether you are willing to believe this or not, the truth is you are 100% responsible for the life you are living right now. You are the sum total of the choices you have made so far. If you are wondering why you would create all the undesirable things in your life, then let me tell you why. You have created them in ignorance. No one taught you that every choice you make influences the outcome of your life. A series of bad choices leads to what the average person describes as "bad luck."

Practicing radical self-love is all about assuming radical responsibility for your life. I am not saying that you have to blame yourself for every single negative thing that has happened to you. All I am saying is the moment you point the finger at someone or something else, you make yourself powerless. You become a victim of circumstances, and when you are a victim there isn't much you can do to change the situation. You are at the mercy of others. Is that how you want to live your life?

The only person standing between you and your dream life is YOU! We are often our own worst enemies. We set new goals enthusiastically, and then sabotage our chances of success. If you want to live an extraordinary life, then you have to stop thinking like an ordinary person. Most people live a life of passivity.

They never take responsibility for their life or for who they are. Turning your dreams into a reality begins by stepping into your full power. That can happen only when you start taking radical responsibility for your life. Don't make yourself powerless by believing in the narrative of "poor me." You are an infinitely powerful being – you have the power to turn all your dreams into reality.

FACE YOUR FEARS

The things we are afraid of the most are the things we need to do the most. It is within these challenges that the seeds of massive growth are hidden. You'll never realize what you are truly capable of if you keep pushing all your demons under the rug. They don't go away like that. To make them go away, you have to confront them.

Fear is a primal emotion. Most of the time, fear has nothing to do with the thing or circumstance you are associating it with. Think about all the people in this world who are able to do the thing that scares you so much. If your fear was logical or factual, then everyone in this world would have the same experience with it, but that's not the case.

The worst thing about fear is that it paralyzes your ability to think or act. Your throat becomes dry, your heart starts pounding, and your palms become sweaty. Worst of all, your mind becomes foggy.

It is important to understand that even the most courageous person in the world has fears. Fear is part and parcel of the human experience. The highly courageous person has just learned to deal with it better. The more often you look fear in the eye and overcome it, the more courageous you become. Being courageous is a choice, and so is staying fearful. You have to choose who you want to be. Your fear has nothing to do with actual facts or circumstances. It has everything to do with YOU. You have to face your own self to overcome that monster you fear so much.

It is not an exaggeration to say that everything worthwhile you want is on the other side of fear. Most people don't succeed because they want rewards without making sacrifices. You have to make sacrifices by doing the things you fear or hate doing. There is no way around it. You can either live a life of mediocrity or you can unleash your greatness. To do the latter, you have to go where most people aren't willing to go – inside that deep dark cavern where your deepest fears reside.

Fear can never be overcome by trying to ignore or forget about the things you fear. To overcome fear, you have to look it in the eye and overcome it by applying grit and determination. Also, most people think that they will be able to do what needs to be done only after their fears have completely disappeared. That is again faulty thinking. You have to persist in your efforts by doing what is needed despite the fear.

Fear should never be resisted because you give greater power to it by resisting it. Instead, you have to overcome fear by embracing it fully. Allow yourself to feel the fear, but do what you need to do in spite of what you are feeling.

THE IMPORTANCE OF EMOTIONAL CONTROL

Fear is an emotional reaction to real or imagined threats. It is a crippling emotion. Fear reduces your power to take action if you allow it to control you. The same goes for all emotions. Emotions deepen our experience of life when we are in control of them. But they can cripple and disempower us if we allow our emotions to control us.

Easier said than done – I know! It does take practice to start being in control of your emotions. The good news is that the more frequently you practice, the better you get at it. No one is born with these character traits. Well, some people are indeed a lot more emotionally sensitive than others. To be successful in life, you have to master the skill of handling emotions effectively.

Our success in all spheres of life depends upon our ability to control our emotions. Developing emotional control is essential for steering the wheels of destiny in your favor. Without emotional control, you cannot make good decisions. The foundation of success is built by consistently taking good decisions.

Think about it – The affection and joy you feel when something wonderful happens makes life beautiful. Life will be so bland if you couldn't feel all these beautiful emotions. On the other hand, think about what happens when you are deeply fearful and anxious about something.

If you are like most people, then you'll label the first example as something positive, and the second one as negative. I used to do that as well. On some level, it isn't wrong. However, in reality, things are a lot more nuanced. There are really no undesirable emotions – all emotions are to be felt and experienced in their fullness.

I know this is contrary to what most modern-day coaches will tell you. You are constantly told to think positive and stay away from "negative" thoughts. It's like asking someone to not think of a pink elephant. The moment you tell someone not to think about it, all they can see inside their mind's eye is a pink elephant. Also, this idea that certain parts of us are undesirable or certain emotions are to be refrained from is a flawed concept.

Everything in nature has its own purpose and significance. We wouldn't have been endowed with these universal human emotions if they didn't have a purpose. Besides, it isn't just you but every single human being on the planet who experiences this full spectrum of human emotions.

You don't need to resist emotions like anger, disgust, fear, or sadness. You need to embrace them. By embracing them, you'll allow yourself to see what your core is trying to tell you through these emotions. For instance, the part that is fearful of making that dreaded phone call may be trying to protect you from the pain of rejection that you felt the last time you did something similar. Once you start realizing that these emotions and those parts of you from whom they stem aren't your enemies but your allies, everything changes.

Instead of putting all your energy into resisting them, you can listen to them. It is amazing how these monsters that we fear so much dwindle and diminish once we stop putting so much energy into resisting them. Embracing all aspects of yourself is the only effective strategy for creating your dream life.

THE EMOTIONAL MASTERY QUIZ

This quiz will help you understand whether you are in control of your emotions or they are in control of you. It will help you understand how much work you need to do. Again, this is not about beating yourself up for your shortcomings. Use the results of this quiz as a tool of empowerment. No matter where you are in life, you have the power to change your destiny.

Creating the life of your dreams and becoming the person you want to be is entirely in your own hands. It doesn't matter what your results turn out to be – the only thing that matters is what you do with them. I always say this and I am going to repeat this one more time: transformation begins with self-awareness and a firm decision to change. Who you have been so far doesn't have to determine who you are going to be from this day onward. You are the only one who has complete power over you – exercise it constructively to become who you have always wanted to be.

I would recommend that you take this quiz after every few months, or maybe annually, to see how much you are in charge of your emotions. Sometimes we are doing a lot worse than we think we are, and at other times, we are actually doing better than we realize. Quizzes like these are excellent for developing greater self-awareness and for acquiring an objective view of how things are.

For each question, give yourself a score on a scale of 0-4. This is what each number indicates: 0 = strongly disagree, 1 = disagree, 2 = neutral, 3 = agree, 4 = strongly agree. Use the scoring guide at the end of this quiz to understand your results.

1. At least 90% of the time, you feel calm and collected.
2. You don't take important decisions when emotions are high. Like, when you are extremely happy and excited or extremely sad and dejected.
3. You think rationally even under pressure.
4. You have mastered the art of thriving on challenges.
5. You don't fear change.
6. You are extremely resilient.
7. You feel negative emotions, but they don't bog you down for too long (not any more than a few hours).
8. You generally don't do or say anything in a state of anger that you'll regret later.

9. You can't remember the last time you had an emotional outburst.
10. When things get challenging, you're the one who tells others to stay calm.
11. When challenges come up, you immediately start thinking about solutions.
12. You firmly believe that there is a solution to every problem. You are fully committed to finding the solution every time you encounter a problem.
13. Others think of you as a positive and uplifting person to be around.
14. You are extremely optimistic.
15. You keep your eyes fixed on the light at the end of the tunnel no matter how dark things are looking.
16. You genuinely believe every challenge is an opportunity to grow and become better.
17. You believe you have the power to weather any storm and emerge victorious on the other end.
18. You don't get too excited about your wins even though you know how to celebrate them.
19. Disappointments and setbacks can never hold you down for too long.
20. After each setback, you come back stronger and more determined to win.
21. You believe you are 100% responsible for your life and everything in it.
22. You believe your happiness is your responsibility alone.

23. You know and fully understand that happiness is a skill that can be learned.
24. You are always in a good mood.
25. You laugh and smile very frequently.
26. You know how to fill each day with joy and beauty.
27. You go to bed with gratitude in your heart.
28. You are grateful to be living your best life right now.
29. You know how to truly enjoy the company of your loved ones.
30. Your loved ones like having you around.

Your Total Score: _____

SCORING GUIDE

Use this guide to understand your results.

100-120 – You have really mastered your emotions. You are doing very well. Emotional mastery is the key to success in all areas of life. Make a note of all those statements where your scores were lower. These are areas where you can grow more. Personal development is a never-ending process. You can always grow more and become more.

The human potential for growth is infinite. This is a wonderful thing – the more you become, the more you can have and enjoy life! Never put a cap on what's possible – stay committed to your personal development and keep growing.

70-100 – You have mastered your emotions to a large extent. This is great! Now, it is time to identify what your major weaknesses are. Check your scores to find out your weaknesses. The statements where you scored the lowest will show you the areas where you need to focus on improving. Don't let this information bog you down. Instead, use it as a tool of empowerment.

Most people don't dare to take an honest look at themselves. You are already doing something that the masses never do. By knowing your weaknesses, you can work on them until they become your strengths. Keep in mind that happiness and emotional control are learnable skills. You have the power to master your emotions and live a life of great happiness.

>70 – You struggle with your emotions. They often get the better of you. The good news is you do have the ability to control your emotions. It is a skill that anyone can learn. It doesn't matter what your starting point is, you can reach your destination if you are committed to it. Identify the statements where you scored the lowest. These are your blind spots. Knowing, admitting, and embracing your weaknesses is the most important step in the journey of transformation.

In the rest of this chapter, I am going to share with you practical tools, tips, ideas, and methods that will help you with emotional mastery. Be sure to read everything attentively and do all the exercises. Always remember that happiness and emotional control are skills that can be learned. You can master your emotions if you are fully committed to making it happen.

THE ART AND SCIENCE OF MASTERING YOUR EMOTIONS

The quality of your life is determined by the quality of your emotions. Hence, emotional mastery is absolutely essential for creating and living a fulfilling life.

I want to share with you practical tools, tips, methods, and strategies that you can immediately start practicing. Understanding things theoretically is not enough for gaining mastery over your emotions. You get results only by practicing what I am sharing with you in this chapter. The more frequently you practice, the better you'll get at it.

Deep Breathing

What happens when you are in a state of fear or anxiety? Your breathing becomes shallow and your throat begins to feel dry. The best and the most effective way to deal with a panic attack is by gently pulling your mind away from the thoughts that are causing you anxiety or fear and focusing your attention entirely on your breath. Simply close your eyes and start observing the inflow and outflow of each breath.

Observe how each breath is flowing inside your nose – visualize and feel it spreading inside your body. As the breath is spreading inside your body, feel each cell of your body getting illuminated with positivity, hope, and joy. As you breathe out, visualize all the fear and negativity getting expelled in the form of a ball of black energy leaving your body.

If it is difficult for you to do this visualization, then you can also just count 1-8 for each breath that is going in and 1-8 for each breath that is going out. So with each inhalation, you'll count 1-2-3-4-5-6-7-8. With each exhalation, you'll count 1-2-3-4-5-6-7-8. Breathe deeply from your stomach and not just from your chest. With each inhalation, your chest and stomach should expand fully. With each exhalation, your chest and stomach should contract completely.

You can also combine the counting exercise with the visualization practice to enhance your focus further. If you feel comfortable doing just the visualization or just the counting exercise, then that is also good.

Exercise

Take a few minutes to practice deep breathing in the manner I have explained above. Moving forward, devote at least five minutes every morning and evening to practice deep breathing. If you start doing this right after waking up and immediately before going to bed, you'll benefit tremendously.

I would also encourage you to get in the habit of practicing it whenever possible. I mean in addition to your morning and evening practice. Yes, you can also do it with your eyes open when it is not possible for you to close your eyes. Closing the eyes helps in focusing better. But when doing so is not an option just do the best you can with your eyes open.

It is especially useful whenever you are feeling anxious, fearful, or perplexed. Just bring your mind into the present moment and focus on your breath. You'll immediately start feeling calm, centered, and more grounded.

Create a statement of commitment to incorporate this practice into your daily routine.

I commit to

_____

Reframing

This is my favorite strategy for dealing with challenging life situations. No two people have the exact same reaction to the same situation. This is because no two people have the exact same mental framework for assessing and understanding a situation.

Our mental frameworks are built through the life experiences we have had and from the conditioning we receive growing up. Most people don't realize that their reaction to a situation isn't the only way one can respond to it. If you want, you can completely reframe things, thereby, transforming your perception of the situation and your reaction to it.

Let me explain this more clearly with an example. Two twin brothers grew up in an extremely abusive household. One becomes a massively successful businessman who contributes to and establishes charities that protect abused children. The other brother becomes an alcoholic who eventually dies from a drug overdose.

Both brothers grew up in the exact same circumstances and faced the exact same challenges, yet they went on to live completely different lives as adults. What is the reason for this?

This is because the successful brother used the challenges to fuel his desire for a better life. The drug-addict brother perceived himself as a victim of circumstances. Hence, he never made the effort to turn the wheels of destiny in his favor.

You can either allow your challenges to bog you down or you can use them to fuel your dreams and passions. You can either be a victim of your circumstances or you can be the one who uses every obstacle to evolve into a higher version of yourself.

The moment you start blaming anyone or anything outside of yourself, you give your power away. It is better to focus on how you can turn your adversities into abundance. You have the power to do it. Once you reframe your perception of the challenging situation, you can identify the blessing that is hidden inside it. Nothing negative can ever happen to you when you are determined to turn every challenging situation into something positive and favorable.

The thing that helps me the most is to always remember that I am here to learn and grow. No matter what situation comes up in life, I can always learn, grow, and become better. By adopting such a mindset, you can make the best of whatever cards you get dealt.

Exercise

Write down a negative situation that bothers you a lot.

_____

_____

_____

Now, think of the blessing that can come out of this situation. Identify how you can learn from this situation and grow into a finer version of yourself. Write everything down in the space below.

_____

_____

_____

_____

_____

_____

Moving forward, what actions are you going to take to turn the challenging situation into a blessing? Write down at least five action items in the space below with at least one being something you are going to do immediately within the next seven days.

_____

_____

_____

_____

_____

_____

7

MAKE THE TIME TO NURTURE YOURSELF DAILY

"With every act of self-care your authentic self gets stronger, and the critical, fearful mind gets weaker. Every act of self-care is a powerful declaration: I am on my side, I am on my side, each day I am more and more on my own side."

— SUSAN WEISS BERRY

I was about to title this chapter "take the time to nurture yourself daily" and then it occurred to me that "take" sounds like you are taking something away from your schedule. Self-care is a gift that you give to yourself. Hence, the word "make" fits in better here – you DESERVE to "make" the time for yourself every single day. You are worthy and deserving of your own love.

I know it is hard for a lot of people. Society constantly bombards us with the idea that making time for ourselves is selfish. We start feeling like any time we are making for ourselves is time that we are taking away from our family and loved ones. Nothing can be farther from the truth.

Taking excellent care of one's own self is not only the most important act of unconditional love, but it is also a moral responsibility. When you don't make the time to look after your own needs, you start expecting others to fill your empty cup. As I said earlier, no one can ever give you what you don't have for yourself.

Ignoring your own needs doesn't serve anyone. If you are constantly prioritizing other people's needs at the expense of your own, it will eventually make you resentful. No one understands you and your needs better than you. You have to do what is necessary for you whether anyone else agrees with it or not. That being said, I have always found that loved ones tend to be very supportive if we explain properly why we need some separate "me-time." If you are surrounded by people who don't want to understand this need of yours or they simply refuse to be supportive, then it may be important to take a deeper look at those relationships.

Either way, you can never please everyone in this world. No one can ever fulfill your needs completely unless you learn to give yourself the fulfillment you are seeking. Other people can add to your joy, happiness, and bliss. If you are waiting for them to fill your pitcher in its entirety, then you must realize that it is just too much to ask for from any human being. You are setting yourself up for disappointment.

HOW TO MAKE TIME FOR YOURSELF NO MATTER HOW BUSY YOU ARE

If you are one of those people who is so busy that you have no time to look after yourself, it is high time you take a step back and start evaluating how your constant busyness is impacting you and your life. We live in a society where being busy or at least claiming to be busy is often seen as a badge of honor. Ask any person if they have time for this or that, and they'll retaliate by saying how busy they are.

Take care of yourself

There is a difference between being busy and being productive. You could be slaving away for 15 hours a day, but if you are not performing at an optimum level, your results won't be commensurate with the toil you are going through.

You don't need to work more hours to be productive. You can get more done in a shorter amount of time if you are mentally, emotionally, and physically performing at your peak level. It is very hard to be productive when one is constantly feeling tired or burnt out. Self-care is not a waste of time or for that matter a luxury. It is an absolute necessity! You won't expect your phone to serve you without charging it every day. Why would you expect your body, mind, and emotions to serve you if you are not doing anything to intentionally replenish your energy levels every day?

Self-care is the most productive thing you can do as it enables you to be more effective and efficient throughout the day. If you want to be highly energetic and extremely productive, then you must take excellent care of yourself. You don't have to take my word for it. For the next 21 days, just follow everything I am sharing in this chapter. If it doesn't change your life for the better, then you can come back to me and tell me how wrong I am. But I can promise you that won't happen!

When your cup is full, you show up stronger and more effective in all areas of life. Self-care leads to self-improvement, and relentless self-improvement is the master key for realizing all your life goals. Keep in mind that you can never experience authentic self-love without intense self-care. Your most important responsibility is to look after yourself.

You are the only one who stays with you eternally. Hence, the relationship you have with yourself is always going to be the most important relationship you can invest in. The more you invest in your relationship with yourself, the stronger you become. Self-care is an excellent investment of your time and energy into YOU.

On that note, let us discuss some practical ways in which you can schedule time for daily self-care in your routine.

Allocate Some Time Where You Belong Only to You

If you have never before prioritized your needs, then chances are you may not get the most enthusiastic response from your near and dear ones if you suddenly tell them you need some time by yourself. It is normal for humans to resist change. When we make dramatic changes to our lives and self, it can make the people around us uncomfortable. They may become fearful of losing their relationship with you, but if they truly love you, they'll eventually understand.

People are also often a lot more supportive if you get them involved in some way. For instance, you can ask them for help with performing some of your responsibilities. Explain to them just how much you'll appreciate their help if they can take care of some things for you so you can use that time to recharge yourself. Never say something like you need a break from your relationship as that can make others feel threatened which would give rise to conflict.

Instead, focus on telling them how their support of your self-care routine enriches your life. Focus on explaining to them how taking care of your own needs will help you be a more pleasant and enjoyable person to be around. If they accept the offer of helping you, be sure to appreciate their efforts by complimenting them generously. Never take anyone for granted. By showing your gratitude and appreciation, you increase the chances of winning over their constant support.

If you live by yourself and you are responsible only for yourself, then you won't have to face this challenge. Either way, make sure that you are spending some time completely cut off from the world.

Use this time to connect with yourself by doing something that replenishes and recharges you. For instance, you can spend time meditating, reading inspiring books, working out, etc. Try to switch off your phone, computer, television, and all other sources of information in your environment. It will help you listen to the voice of your own soul loud and clear.

Exercise

Write down all the self-care practices that you enjoy doing. These should be things that help you feel refreshed, rejuvenated, and replenished.

What can you do to reduce your stress levels? Who can you ask for help?

Wake Up a Little Earlier

I am not suggesting that you should wake up at 4 or 5 am every day. You just need to wake up early enough to spend some time charging your batteries for the day ahead. You don't want to get out of bed and start your day in a reactive mode. Taking the time to prepare for the day will help you feel you are in charge. If you wake up late and start the day in reactive mode, it feels as if everything is spiraling out of control.

You want to have at least half an hour where you can just be by yourself and do what is important to you in that time. If you can schedule an hour or more, then that's even better! Waking up just half an hour earlier than usual to practice some self-care is guaranteed to dramatically change your life.

To wake up early, you have to go to bed early. Instead of making a drastic change to your schedule, start by going to bed just one minute earlier than usual and wake up just one minute earlier than usual. Over the next 60 days, increase this time by one minute every day. By the end of the 60-day period, you will be waking up half an hour earlier. It is easier to implement small incremental changes that compound over time to create dramatic results.

When implementing new changes, always remember the good old proverb that slow and steady wins the race.

Exercise

How much time would you like to devote every morning to your self-care routine?

Do you need to wake up earlier to have some undisturbed "me time" every day? What should be your wake-up time? What changes are you going to make to your schedule to accommodate your new self-care practices?

· · ·

Take Small Breaks Throughout the Day

Taking short breaks throughout the day to indulge in some self-care will definitely improve your productivity. It doesn't matter whether your work involves being an executive, a CEO, or a housewife, you do need to take regular breaks. Breaks are essential for refreshing your mind and recharging your batteries.

By being more intentional with your time, you can use your breaks to replenish your energy. The keyword here is "intentional." The time you spend mindlessly scrolling social media won't help you feel recharged and replenished. On the contrary, it will drain you and leave you feeling depleted. I am sure you already know the feeling I am talking about.

Personally, I like to use the Pomodoro Technique to maximize my productivity throughout the day. It is a time management method developed by a man called Francesco Cirillo (Cirillo Company, n.d.). The technique involves working in spurts of 25 minutes followed by a five-minute break. In the 25-minute period, you cut out all distractions and focus only on the job at hand. It is easier for the mind to concentrate intensely when the goal is to do it only for 25 minutes. When the mind knows that you are going to get a five-minute break at the end of the 25-minute period, it cooperates better.

Each 25-minute spurt is known as a pomodoro. At the end of four pomodoros, you can take a longer break of 20-30 minutes. During the breaks, it is best to do something that gets you to move your body. For instance, you can take a walk or maybe even do some light stretching. Also, use the breaks to drink some water and grab a healthy snack if you need one.

The Pomodoro Technique can be used for performing all kinds of tasks. Whether you are mowing the lawn or writing a business report, you can use it to be more productive and efficient. It is especially helpful when working on difficult tasks that seem overwhelming. There are many websites and apps that can help you with tracking your pomodoros. Just find one you like and start timing yourself. You can also do it the old-fashioned way by using an alarm clock and manually tracking your progress on paper. Do what works best for you.

The only thing I would caution you against doing is mindlessly scrolling your phone during breaks. I am not saying that you can never do that, but we all know how one minute of "just checking updates" turns into an hour or two of mindlessly browsing online. If you want, you can set aside some time every day where you get to freely browse the web. It must be done once all the important tasks for the day have been. Always be intentional with your time.

I would also recommend that you impose a time cap on how long you are allowed to mindlessly browse the internet every day. For instance, you can give yourself 30 minutes every day where you can do things like watch TV or mindlessly browse news feeds. At the end of the 30 minutes, your alarm will go off, and you'll leave whatever you were doing.

Using this strategy will help you stay in charge of your time. You won't feel guilty because you'd know you have earned that time to do as you please. That being said, be very careful to not let yourself fall into the trap of "just one more minute" when the alarm goes off. One minute easily becomes five, 20, 30 minutes, and so on.

The feeling of not being in control of your actions induces a gnawing sense of guilt. To experience self-love, you have to practice self-discipline. You have to get into the habit of doing what is best for you instead of caving into the temptation of doing whatever you feel like in the moment.

Exercise

Which self-care practices would you like to do during your short breaks?

Important Self-Care Practices that You Should Implement in Your Life

In this section, I am going to share with you some of the most important self-care practices that are essential for leading a happy and fulfilling life. You don't have to implement all of them immediately. In fact, I would advise you against it as you'll likely end up feeling overwhelmed. Smaller changes made gradually over a longer period often create better transformations than drastic changes made in a short time.

I would suggest that you identify just one thing that is most out of balance for you right now and focus on fixing that. Pick something that is going to have a very high impact on all areas of your life. For instance, getting enough sleep is the most important self-care practice because if you are not getting proper rest, you won't be able to function at peak energy levels.

Lack of sleep also takes a massive toll on the body and mind. It can even offset the benefits of healthy eating and regular exercise. Getting proper sleep will hugely impact all other areas of your life as you'll have more energy for doing everything better. This is just one example. Maybe your situation is different. Like, if you are suffering from lethargy, then working out every day may get you the highest return on investment.

In short, pick one thing that would impact your life the most and stick with it for at least a month. In fact, I would say 90 days. In my experience, it takes much longer than 21 or 30 days to really form a habit. At the end of the 90-day period, you can pick something else that you want to focus exclusively on. The interesting thing is if you make one positive change, then it will automatically have a domino effect on all the other areas of your life.

For instance, going to the gym daily will motivate you to eat healthier. You'll find yourself making better food choices simply because you don't want to sabotage your progress in the gym. This is a wonderful thing. You really don't have to force yourself to adopt all the healthy self-care practices at once. Just focus on one thing at a time. As you make progress, maintain the habit you have already built and then keep adding new ones on top of it.

Proper Sleep

For a very long time, I treated sleep in the same way as most youngsters do. Yes, I thought it was something optional. It's only much later in life that I began realizing the toll that chronic sleep deprivation takes on the mind and body. Now, I am not suggesting that every single person should sleep a specific number of hours every night. In my opinion, that kind of advice is good as saying everyone in the world needs to eat the exact same diet.

The truth is people have different physiological and psychological makeup. The amount of sleep you need may be completely different from what I need. You are the only one who knows what the optimum amount of sleep for you is. I would strongly recommend maintaining a sleep journal where you note down the amount of sleep you are getting each night along with a short note about how you were feeling when you woke up.

I would also recommend noting down the time when you are falling asleep and the time when you are waking up. In my experience, when we are going to bed and when we are waking up are far more important factors in determining the quality of rest we receive than merely counting hours.

If I sleep at 3 am and wake up at 11 am, I feel extremely lethargic and tired even though technically I have had 8 hours of sleep. On the other hand, I wake up refreshed and energetic when I go to bed at 10 pm and wake up at 4 am. Technically, it is less sleep but, in my experience, the hours don't matter nearly as much as when we are going to bed and when we are waking up.

Ideally, our sleep schedule should be in sync with nature's rhythm of day and night. To learn more, you can read about the body clock system that Chinese medicine talks about. Ayurveda also discusses this subject in depth. If you research "dinacharya," you'll find out what Ayurveda recommends for a healthy daily routine. I would advise you to educate yourself in this area and then craft out a sleep schedule that works best for you.

Exercise

How would you rate your sleep quality on a scale of 1-10, with 1 being very low and 10 being exceptionally good?

What would your ideal sleep schedule look like – at what time do you see yourself going to bed every night and waking up each morning?

**Start maintaining a sleep journal where you record when you went to bed, when you woke up, and how many hours of sleep you got. Also, take notes about the quality of sleep you are having.**

Healthy Diet

I don't believe in there being just one ideal diet that everyone in the world should stick to. Your ideal healthy diet depends a lot upon your health status, fitness goals, lifestyle, and other unique factors.

In general, I can tell you that it is best to cut out all food items that have colors, additives, and other chemicals. Try to stay away from ready-to-eat food items as much as possible. Instead, focus on eating fresh fruits, vegetables, and whole grains.

You are the best person to know what kind of diet works for you. If you really aren't sure how to create a good diet plan for yourself, then you can consult a professional fitness trainer or a qualified dietician to help create your custom diet plan.

Again, my recommendation here is that you be a lot more intentional with your choices. Opt for natural and unprocessed food items as much as possible. Stay away from chemical-laden items.

Exercise

What does your ideal diet plan look like? Take help from a professional if you aren't sure about how to create a custom plan for yourself.

Start maintaining a food journal where you are writing down everything you are eating in a day. The simple act of recording your food choices will make you a lot more conscious of what you are putting in your mouth. Don't put off doing this until a time in the future when you are hoping to get your diet on track. You need to start this process right now!

Regular Exercise

Moving your body regularly is absolutely essential for maintaining good health. The human body is not designed to remain in a sedentary position all day every day. I am not suggesting that you must get a gym membership if that's not something you want to do. I would say it is far more important to get in the habit of making healthier choices throughout the day than devoting an hour in the gym. The latter is important, but what you are doing the rest of the 23 hours is even more important.

Being a healthy and fit person requires thinking differently. You have to train yourself to make better choices throughout the day. For instance, take the stairs at work instead of the elevator. Consider walking to places instead of driving everywhere. Being healthy and fit is a lifestyle and not just an activity confined to a specific hour of the day.

On weekends and holidays, you can invite all your loved ones to do some activity together. Like, you can all ride a bike or go hiking. You can also play sports together. Like, volleyball, basketball, etc. Think creatively and plan activities that you know everyone will enjoy and that everyone you are inviting has the physical capacity to participate in.

Exercise

Write down at least five things you can implement in your daily life that will help you move your body more. For example, going to the gym, taking the stairs, playing volleyball on the weekends, etc.

Slowly start adding these activities to your daily routine.

_____

_____

_____

_____

_____

_____

_____

_____

Regular Relaxation and Meditation

I would highly recommend that you regularly take the time to relax your body, mind, and spirit. It can be anything from weekly massages to daily five-minute meditation.

I would strongly suggest that you add meditation to your daily routine. You can find a simple guided meditation online that you truly resonate with and start using it every day. You can also try out different types of meditation depending on how you are feeling each day.

Meditation helps make you really present in the moment and that is the key to authentic happiness and radical self-love.

By being fully present in the moment, you can easily love and accept yourself on all levels.

A lot of people claim that they just cannot meditate. If that sounds like you, then you are likely wondering how you can meditate when your mind jumps around too much to let you sit still. Believe it or not, that's everyone's mind.

Yes, even the most seasoned meditation practitioners have a monkey mind. They have just trained themselves to deal with it better. If you stop fighting your mind's tendency to jump from one thought or idea to another, and, instead, accept whatever comes up, it will stop troubling you so much.

You always want to think of thoughts as waves arising on the ocean floor. Let them arise and subside on their own. You'll be amazed by how quickly the negative thoughts disappear once you stop fighting against them.

Just try out meditating for the next 14 days. You'll be amazed by the benefits – I promise!

Exercise

What are the activities that you can implement in your daily life to relax your body, mind, and spirit? Write down at least five suggestions.

Once you have your list ready, start implementing each suggestion one at a time.

8

PRACTICING THE ART OF HAPPINESS

"Happiness is a choice you make and a skill you develop. The mind is just as malleable as the body."

— NAVAL RAVIKANT

Staying happy and joyful is not something that just happens to you without you putting in any effort. It is a skill that you develop through deliberate practice. But first, you have to consciously decide to be happy. Yes, being happy is a matter of choice and decision.

Most people think that happiness is something that just happens on its own. Nothing can be farther from the truth. You can put 10 people in the same situation and each one will respond to it differently. Some people will find what is wonderful about the situation and will choose to be happy. Others will find something negative even in the most favorable set of circumstances.

In short, people who have developed the skill of happiness will figure out how to find joy and happiness in all situations. On the other hand, those who have developed the habit of constantly complaining will find a reason to complain about things no matter how well everything is going.

Happiness is, therefore, a matter of perspective. If you want to be happier, then you must commit to cultivating happiness. Slowly, your perspective will start shifting, and you'll become the type of person who sees the good in every situation.

HAPPINESS BEGINS WITH ACCEPTANCE

The feeling of unhappiness arises only when we allow ourselves to think that something is missing from life. This is why a person can be extremely happy living in a mud hut with a leaking ceiling and another person can be miserable even while living inside a grand luxurious palace. Happiness has very little to do with our outer circumstances – it is dependent largely upon our internal state.

If you'd allow yourself to believe that something is missing from your life, then you'll automatically feel unhappy. Instead, if you can get yourself to accept life just the way it is, then you can be fully present in the here and now. The present moment is where happiness is experienced in its full glory.

Now, I am not suggesting that you should become smug and not aspire for more in your life. Absolutely not! I am all for constant growth and improvement. The idea here is to aspire for more while being grateful for what you already have.

Whoever you are, whatever you are experiencing, and everything you have right now is the sum total of all your past decisions. Since the past is history, there is nothing you can do about it. Your power lies in the here and now. You can change the future you are creating for yourself by making better choices today.

The same idea applies to self-acceptance. You accept who you are today with unconditional love and gratitude while constantly aspiring to be better. You don't have to be disdainful towards yourself or your life in order to be a better person and experience a better life.

Gratitude is undoubtedly the perfect antidote to sadness and negativity. By being grateful for all the blessings you have in your life, you can immediately shift your perspective. Even if you think there is nothing to be grateful for in your life right now that can never be true. If you have food on the table, a roof over your head, and this book in your hand – you already have a lot to be grateful for.

The problem with us humans is that we often don't value what we have until we no longer have it. If you feel there is nothing in your life to be grateful for, then that means you are taking a lot of things for granted. If you start counting all the big and small things that are going well in your life right now, then you'll definitely come up with a long list of things to be grateful for.

Exercise

Create a list of at least 10 things that you are grateful for in your life right now. Be sure to include both big and small things.

_____

_____

_____

_____

_____

_____

_____

_____

_____

_____

Write down at least 10 things you have in your life right now that, in the past, were things you wished for. It can be something small like a favorite outfit you were finally able to buy or something big like the career of your dreams. I am sure if you think hard enough, you'll easily come up with at least 10 things that were once a dream but are now part of your reality.

From now on, every morning write down at least three things you are grateful for. Challenge yourself to come up with something new and different every day. Be sure to include both big and small things in your list. Even having a pen to write with or a computer to type on are things to be grateful for!

By starting your day with gratitude, you'll train yourself to retain a more positive attitude throughout the day.

I'll also suggest that whenever you are feeling low or negative, you create a list of at least 10 things you are grateful for. Gratitude truly is the most powerful practice for immediately shifting your mood and mindset. Think of it like this – when you are feeling negative or depressed, your head is turned in the wrong direction. Gratitude immediately turns your head in the right direction helping you focus on all your blessings and all the positivity that surrounds you.

THE IMPORTANCE OF ENERGY MANAGEMENT

Time management is a hot topic. Everyone wants to know how they can manage their time better. There are countless tools and methods that promise to make one more efficient and effective. The problem is time management tools rarely ever work. At least, they never worked for me!

I would create a really demanding timetable for myself, and then I'll fail to stick to it. It is akin to trying to go on a diet. Very soon, you begin feeling like a total failure as forcing yourself to stick to anything brings up a lot of resistance and negativity in your psyche.

Eventually, I came upon this idea of energy management. People always say time is money. Time is regarded as the most valuable resource in the world. My perspective is slightly different. I feel there is only so much energy we have throughout the day and how we allocate tasks depending upon our varying energy levels determines how much fulfillment we'd get out of our day. Efficient energy management is absolutely essential for being happy.

For me, this implies holding a clear distinction in my mind as to which activities deplete my energy reserves and which ones energize me. For instance, working on a business report often leaves me slightly depleted. I have to balance it by engaging in an activity that replenishes my energy reserves. For instance, meditation energizes me. So after working on a business report for 4 hours, I may take a half an hour break to meditate.

I must clarify here that just because an activity requires a depletion or expenditure of energy doesn't mean that it is something bad or negative. Energy is the currency with which we experience life. In the simple process of living life, we do have to expend the energy that we are constantly generating and accumulating. The key to living a fulfilling and happy life lies in realizing which tasks require a higher expenditure of energy and then intentionally balancing them by also engaging in activities that energize you.

It is like driving a car. In the process of driving, you are going to use up fuel – that's not a bad thing. It is simply a necessity and a natural consequence of living life. Just like how you constantly keep refueling the gas tank at regular intervals, you have to do the same thing to the same for building your energy reserves.

For instance, an hour-long run may leave you feeling depleted even though it is excellent for your health and fitness. You can recharge yourself by playing with your children for half an hour (if it is something that helps you feel energized).

This strategy is also excellent for building good habits. Reward is a better teacher than punishment. By constantly rewarding yourself for all the positive actions you are taking, you can program yourself to do more of those good things.

Exercise

Create a list of all the activities that you perform on a typical day. Classify them as "ED" (energy depleting) or "ER" (energy replenishing). Pair each ED activity with an ER activity. This way, you will keep refueling your tank throughout the day.

ASSESS YOUR PRIORITIES

Most people live their life on auto-pilot. They do the same thing day in and day out without thinking much about what they are doing. Mastering the skill of happiness requires intentional living. It is easy to take life for granted when you are feeling you'd be here forever, but we all know human life is defined by its brevity.

In the grand scheme of things, if you just sit down to calculate the length and span of the average human life, you'll realize that none of us have that much time here. I am not saying this to invoke fear in you. I personally feel it is very liberating to realize that none of us are going to be here forever.

If you are afraid of doing certain things because of what other people would think, then I would urge you to look at it from a different perspective. Think about it – 60 or 80 years from now it is likely that none of those people whose opinion you fear so much would be around. Maybe by then, you won't be around as well. When you are on your deathbed would it really seem worthwhile that you gave up your dream because of the opinion of others?

Once you start taking decisions keeping in mind the brevity of human life, it becomes easier to do the things you are afraid of doing. There is only so much time you have here. It is better to live this life in accordance with your core values instead of striving to constantly please others at the expense of your own goals and dreams.

Happiness is something you experience when you are living a life that is true to your core values. Again, knowing your core values is very important for living a fulfilling life. You also need to have a vision for what you want your life to be like and for who you want to be. Of course, nothing is set in stone.

As you keep growing, your goals, dreams, and vision will also likely evolve and change. But at any given point in time, you do need to know who you want to be and how you want to live your life.

Exercise

What are the things you want to do that you are not doing right now because of fear or uncertainty? Create a list, then pick one thing that is most important to you right now, and just do it! If you can't do it right now, then give yourself a deadline (a specific date and time) by which you MUST do it.

EXPECT LESS FROM OTHERS AND MORE FROM YOURSELF

Expecting too much from others is the number one happiness killer. A person who expects too much from others just cannot be happy. No matter how close someone is to you, they are an individual in their own right. You can't control their behavior and actions. Your expectations not only sabotage your peace of mind, but they also negatively impact your relationship with the other person.

When you are doing something for others, it should be from your heart. Never do anything expecting something in return. The act should be its own reward. This way, you aren't dependent on someone else's actions to give you what you need. You already have the peace and contentment you need. Any acknowledgment or gift the other person gives you becomes a bonus. Hence, you are better able to appreciate what they are giving you.

Being happy means being self-reliant. You have to train yourself to depend upon yourself to meet all your needs. Of course, you should ask others for help whenever you need it. You can tell them exactly what they can do for you, but beyond that don't harness any expectations. Whether the person chooses to meet your needs or not is entirely upon them. You have to do what's best for you and sometimes this means walking away from a relationship where your needs are not being met.

By practicing self-care rituals and doing things that meet your needs, you keep your own cup full. Other people can add to that happiness, but you aren't dependent on anyone to get your needs met.

Exercise

What are your expectations from others that are currently not being met?

_____

_____

_____

_____

How can you fulfill those needs on your own?

Are your communicating your needs clearly in your relationships? What action do you need to take in the relationships where your needs are currently not being met?

HELP OTHERS

Ultimately, life is measured by the impact we have on others. Helping others unconditionally is one of the most rewarding things in life. When you do something for someone else without any hidden agenda, it does something to you at a very deep level. You are able to double up your fulfillment because you get to feel the fulfillment of the other person along with your own.

"You have not lived a perfect day unless you've done something for someone who will never be able to repay you."

— RUTH SMELTZER

As human beings, we are social creatures. We thrive in communities. We need each other to function effectively as a society. At the spiritual level as well, we are all connected. When we do something good for another soul, we are also doing good for ourselves. Besides, the Universe rewards every positive act. Whatever we give comes back to us multiplied

That being said, you should never do something for someone if you are looking for rewards or even acknowledgment. Do it because it feels right and because it is what you genuinely want to do. Only then, it is guaranteed that your good deeds will be rewarded. When you are not attached to the outcome, it doesn't really matter whether you receive something back or not. But you will!

This attitude is the master key to living a blessed and happy life. By doing good, you attract good things into your life. When you are not expecting anything and you receive a reward for your good deeds, it makes you very happy. This is so much better than expecting too much and feeling disappointed because you didn't receive what you wanted.

You don't always have to do big things to create a huge impact on someone's life. Sometimes a small act of kindness like a heartfelt smile or an uplifting compliment can make someone's day.

Give happiness to others and you will automatically become a happier person. Do things for others without expecting anything in return. Perform acts of kindness out of the goodness of your own heart. You'll be amazed by how incredible it feels to put a smile on someone else's face. Don't let this be an isolated act you do once in a while. Develop the habit of helping others unconditionally on a regular basis.

Exercise

Think of one person whom you can help right now. Write down exactly how you can help them. Once you have the answer, just take action on it!

CONCLUSION

I hope you have enjoyed this journey toward greater self-love. If you completed all the exercises, then I am sure you have undergone a shift in how you feel about yourself and your life. If you haven't completed all the exercises, then I would urge you to go back and complete them.

Reading a book is powerful, but to change your life you have to take action. By reading a book, you can feed your mind new ideas, but unless you put things to practice the information you are absorbing won't benefit you much.

Also, don't let this be one of those books that you read once, and then it just gathers dust on your bookshelf. Keep coming back to this workbook. Maintain a journal where you can practice the exercises again after a few weeks or months.

Compare them to everything you had written in this workbook. I am sure you'll be amazed by the progress you make. Keep repeating this process every couple of months.

Every time you come back to this workbook, you'll develop new insights and perspectives. You'll learn more about yourself and about your life. The content of the book remains the same but it is you who will evolve more by the next time you come back to this book. As you grow, your capacity to understand and perceive things at a different level also transforms. You start observing things that weren't obvious to you before.

As human beings, we have infinite potential for love and growth. The more you grow as a human being, the greater self-love you'll experience. All relationships require time and effort. This is just as true for your relationship with yourself as it is true for your relationships with others. You have to nurture your own self if you want to have a deeply fulfilling relationship with yourself. No relationship is as rewarding as a lifetime of romance with one's own self. Whatever investment you are making in this one relationship right now is guaranteed to be totally worthwhile in long run!

I would urge you to continue the practices that you have adopted through this workbook. If you want to add something extra, then I would suggest checking out my "I Am Capable Project - Daily Affirmations" book series. In those books, you'll find unique affirmations that you can add to your morning, afternoon, and evening routines respectively.

Be sure to invest in yourself every single day. Nothing is more powerful than falling in love with yourself over and over again.

Sincerely,

S. S. Leigh

REFERENCES

Banks, T. (n.d.). *Tyra Banks quotes.* BrainyQuote. Retrieved October 23, 2022, from https://www.brainyquote.com/quotes/tyra_banks_452188

Berry, S. W. (n.d.). *A quote by Susan Weiss Berry.* Goodreads. Retrieved October 23, 2022, from https://www.goodreads.com/quotes/10377421

Brown, B. (n.d.). **Quoted in** *50 self-love quotes to boost your confidence and Lift your spirits.* Good Housekeeping. Retrieved October 23, 2022, from https://www.goodhousekeeping.com/life/g38333580/self-love-quotes/

Jones, A. M. (2020, October 4). *New Study suggests handwriting engages the brain more than typing.* CTVNews. Retrieved October 23, 2022, from https://www.ctvnews.ca/health/

new-study-suggests-handwriting-engages-the-brain-more-than-typing-1.5132542

Kanter, R. M. (n.d.). *Rosabeth Moss Kanter quotes*. Brainy-Quote. Retrieved October 23, 2022, from https://www.brainyquote.com/quotes/rosabeth_moss_kanter_390507

Maxwell, J. C. (2009). *How Successful People Think: Change Your Thinking, Change Your Life*. Center Street.

Owen, S. (n.d.). *A quote from Resilient Me*. Goodreads. Retrieved October 23, 2022, from https://www.goodreads.com/quotes/9064580

Pareto principle. Wikipedia. (n.d.). Retrieved October 23, 2022, from https://en.wikipedia.org/wiki/Pareto_principle

The Pomodoro® Technique. Cirillo Company. (n.d.). Retrieved October 23, 2022, from https://francescocirillo.com/products/the-pomodoro-technique

Ravikant, N. (n.d.). **Quoted in** *Happiness is a choice*. Almanack of Naval Ravikant. Retrieved October 23, 2022, from https://www.navalmanack.com/almanack-of-naval-ravikant/happiness-is-a-choice

Schwartz, R. (2021). *No Bad Parts: Healing Trauma and Restoring Wholeness with the Internal Family Systems Model*. Sounds True.

Smeltzer, R. (n.d.). *A quote by Ruth Smeltzer*. Goodreads. Retrieved October 23, 2022, from https://www.goodreads.

com/quotes/120222-you-have-not-lived-a-perfect-day-unless-you-ve-done

Williamson, M. (n.d.). Goodreads. Retrieved October 23, 2022, from https://www.goodreads.com/quotes/928

Winfrey, O. (n.d.). *A quote by Oprah Winfrey*. Goodreads. Retrieved October 23, 2022, from https://www.goodreads.com/quotes/2587-when-you-undervalue-what-you-do-the-world-will-undervalue

GOOD WILL

Helping others without expectation of anything in return has been proven to lead to increased happiness and satisfaction in life.

I would love to give you the chance to experience that same feeling during your reading or listening experience today...

All it takes is a few moments of your time to answer one simple question:

<u>Would you make a difference in the life of someone you've never met—without spending any money or seeking recognition for your good will?</u>

If so, I have a small request for you.

If you've found value in your reading or listening experience today, I humbly ask that you take a brief moment right now to leave an honest review of this book. It won't cost you anything but 30 seconds of your time—just a few seconds to share your thoughts with others.

Your voice can go a long way in helping someone else find the same inspiration and knowledge that you have.

Are you familiar with leaving a review for a Kindle, or e-reader book? If so, it's simple:

If you're reading on **Kindle** or an e-reader, simply scroll to the last page of the book and swipe up—the review should prompt from there.

If you're on a **Paperback** or any other physical format of this book, you can find the book page on Amazon (or wherever you bought this) and leave your review right there.

EMOTIONAL REGULATION SKILLS TO OVERCOME TOXIC THINKING AND BEHAVIOR

GET OUT OF YOUR HEAD AND CALM YOUR THOUGHTS WITH PRACTICAL STRATEGIES AND EXERCISES; STOP ANGER, ANXIETY, JEALOUSY, AND INSECURITY

S. S. LEIGH

Learn to use your emotions to think, not think with your emotions.

— ROBERT KIYOSAKI

INTRODUCTION

Emotions are a beautiful thing – they enable us to experience life in all its richness and fullness. Untamed emotions, on the other hand, can cause us enormous distress and suffering. Learning to regulate one's emotions is hands-down the single most important skill one must master in order to live a truly fulfilling life.

From my own experience, I have come to believe that 90% of success in any area of life boils down to one's mindset and ability to control one's emotions. Whether it is business or personal relationships, without emotional control you are likely to keep taking poor decisions that prevent you from getting what you want.

That being said, if you feel your negative emotions are spiraling out of control and you just can't stop thinking obsessively about everything that's not good for you, let me give you an assurance. You are not alone! What you are facing is a very human struggle. No one is born with emotional regulation skills. Of course, it is true that different people have innately different levels of sensitivity. But even then, emotional regulation is a skill one has to master through deliberate and intentional practice.

At this point in my life, everyone thinks that I have always been as calm and composed as I am now. Honestly, I can't help but chuckle. I wish they had seen me when I used to be a nervous wreck struggling to function properly at home and at work. My mind used to be constantly preoccupied with everything that could go wrong. Thanks to such negative thinking, I would be jittery with fear and nervousness 24/7.

Negative thoughts and negative emotions are strongly inter-linked. Trying to determine which one comes first is akin to attempting to solve the classic chicken and egg conundrum. Thoughts and emotions go hand-in-hand. Negative thinking causes a surge of negative emotions and vice versa. This eventually leads to detrimental behavior patterns which prevent one from achieving one's goals and living the kind of life one desires to live.

To change detrimental behavior patterns, you have to work on transforming your thoughts and emotions. The good news is that when you work on transforming your thought patterns, your emotional state also undergoes a change.

Similarly, your emotions undergo a transformation when you become in charge of your emotions. Working on either one of these pays off enormously. In this book, I'm going to show you how to transform both your thoughts and emotions although the focus would be more on working with emotions.

This is because, from my own experience, I can tell you that working on our emotions pays off a lot more heavily than adopting a thought-centric approach. We like to think of ourselves as creatures of logic but, in reality, we are creatures of emotions. As human beings, it is easier for us to suspend logic than to suspend our emotions. There is plenty of research that shows how most of our life is run by our emotions. That isn't a bad thing in itself. The question is what kind of emotions are running our life.

Emotions can give us a powerful motivation to accomplish seemingly impossible feats – something that logic alone can never do to us. For instance, just imagine what a mother would do to save her baby who is trapped inside a burning house. You need that kind of fire and drive to achieve big things in life. It is impossible to foster it through logic alone. Logic is helpful for making sound decisions but you need passion and emotional intensity to achieve great things.

Having negative emotions like anger, fear, or anxiety isn't necessarily a bad thing. It is what you do with them that determines whether these emotions are serving you or acting against you. You can use all your negative emotions for positive action. With the right attitude, negative emotions can serve as the rocket fuel that launches you to achieve your goals.

As human beings, we must experience the full spectrum of emotions. No emotion is to be denied, suppressed, or avoided. In fact, what we resist persists. The goal is to accept, embrace, and experience all your emotions without being negatively impacted by them. If you have no idea right now how that is even possible, don't worry. I am here for you. I'll show you how you can do it.

Mastering and regulating your emotions doesn't imply you'll never experience any negative emotions. A lot of coaches teach this approach but it's not healthy at all. Denying, suppressing, or resisting emotions is akin to stuffing all your clutter into a closet. You close the doors and think all the clutter has been removed from your space. It only lasts until the day the doors of the closet burst open and the clutter spreads everywhere once again. Our emotions work in exactly the same way. Emotional suppression causes a person to blow up at the most unexpected times and inopportune moments.

In this book, I'll show you how you can master your emotions without suppressing, denying, or resisting them. There is no such thing as a quick fix. Emotional mastery requires time, effort, and practice. But the good news is that even a little effort pays huge dividends. Emotional regulation is the most important skill you are ever going to have in your arsenal. Life is a lot simpler and easier when you have control over your emotions.

Emotional regulation is a skill that anyone can develop and master. It doesn't matter what your past has been like. You can acquire emotional mastery even if you have been told your whole life you are "too emotional" for your own good. Everything can be changed. Becoming the person you have always wanted to be is entirely in your own hands. If I can do it, then so can you! As I shared with you earlier, there was a time in my life when I had no control over my emotions. Now, I live life with calmness, composure, and tremendous self-control.

In this book, I have strived to share with you everything I have learned along the way to become the person that I am today. If you'd follow what I am sharing, then you'll get the same results. That's just inevitable!

1

UNDERSTANDING HOW EMOTIONS, THOUGHTS, AND BEHAVIOR ARE INTERCONNECTED

"Thoughts create emotions, emotions create feelings and feelings create behavior. So it's very important that our thoughts are positive, to attract the right people, events and circumstances into our lives."

— AVIS WILLIAMS

To understand how emotions, thoughts, and behavior are interconnected, we have to first define each one. So let us start with the first one – what is an emotion? I think this definition sums it up quite well: "An emotion occurs when there are certain biological, certain experien-

tial, and certain cognitive states which all occur simultaneously." (Mayer, n.d.)

It is safe to assume that emotions are an essential part of the
feedback mechanism of the human psyche. Emotions help
guide our actions or at times misguide our actions (when we
allow our emotions to control us instead of exercising
control over it).

Now, let us look at the definition of thought: "The terms
thought and thinking refer to conscious cognitive processes
that can happen independently of sensory stimulation."
(Wikipedia, n.d.) In other words, thoughts arise of their own
accord. That being said, the experience of certain emotions
can also lead to specific thoughts.

Thoughts and emotions often lead to behavior. "Behavior is
how someone acts. It is what a person does to make something happen, to make something change, or to keep things
the same. Behavior is a response to things that are happening: internally - thoughts and feelings; externally - the environment, including other people." (NSW Health, n.d.)

Since these three are powerfully interlinked, any change to
either of the three would lead to an automatic influence on
the other two. Hence, if we are struggling with negative
thoughts or negative emotions, an intentional positive
change in behavior will impact our thoughts and emotions
as well. In practice, what does this look like?

So let us say you have been feeling overwhelmed by negative thoughts and emotions. You recognize what is going on. In order to change your state, you intentionally schedule an activity that you enjoy. For instance, having a fun day at an amusement park or maybe just going for a walk in your favorite park. Performing an enjoyable activity will automatically have a powerful influence on your mind and your emotions.

Personally, this is my favorite way of changing my state. The effect is almost immediate. Moving your body compels your emotions and thoughts to also shift. If you'll remain stuck at a place while negative thoughts and emotions overwhelm you, it will be very hard to disperse such a state by using mental and emotional strategies alone. Of course, they have their own place and I am not undermining their importance in any way. I feel it is best to combine different strategies together to transform your state.

That being said, you can also impact your behavior by working only on your thoughts or on your emotions. Of course, it will require more effort as getting your mind to think a certain way or your emotions to be channelized in a certain direction is much harder than simply jumping into action. In my experience, techniques for transforming thoughts and emotions work best in conjunction to behavioral modifications. If you do all three, success is guaranteed!

For now, let us say you wanted to work on your thoughts. You can use affirmations to transform your negative thinking. I often advise my clients to write down their negative thoughts on a sheet of paper and then write statements that are exactly the opposite of what they initially wrote down on another sheet of paper. These new positive statements are their affirmations. I suggest tearing down and burning the first sheet and then frequently repeating the new positive affirmations they created.

Affirmations become powerful when they are repeated often. If you can get yourself to feel what you are saying as if it were already true, you will get results very fast. Ideally, affirmations should always be repeated with emotions. However, when you are starting out, it may be hard to get yourself to feel all the emotions. You can use visualization to feel what the words convey. But be patient.

Over time, you will definitely start feeling the truth encapsulated in the words you are repeating. As you can see, transforming your state by using affirmations may take longer than using a positive activity to do the same. Ideally, you want to combine both because you need long-term transformation by changing your thought processes and emotional patterns. In the short term, getting your body moving and engaging in productive activities often turns out to be the most effective strategy. Combined with tools for transforming thought patterns and emotions, it becomes even more effective.

So now, if we were working only on emotions what would it look like? To transform the emotional state, I often advise my clients to use the power of memory. The mind can't tell the difference between what is imagined and what is real. When you are watching a horror movie, your body undergoes the same physiological reactions as what would occur if you were facing a threatening situation in real life. You can use this knowledge to your advantage by intentionally imagining a pleasant scenario or even watching a movie that evokes positive emotions in you.

There are three ways in which you can do this:

- Recall a time in your past when you felt safe, supported, and happy. Go back to that moment in time and relive all the emotions you felt there.
- Think of a scene from a movie or TV show that evokes a strong positive emotional response in you. Watch this scene repeatedly allowing yourself to fully experience the emotions that arise through the experience.
- Create a vision of a personal heaven. Close your eyes and visualize your ideal world where you feel loved, supported, and cared for. Allow yourself to feel all the positive emotions that arise.

Of course, doing these exercises requires more effort as you have to intentionally shift your focus from what is causing you anxiety to what would soothe you. As I said earlier, ideally, you want to combine different techniques to work on your thoughts, emotions, and behavior simultaneously. But I also want you to test out working on each of these aspects individually so you'll see for yourself how working on any one aspect immediately impacts the other two.

If you haven't tested out the techniques I shared with you, go back and re-read this section and test out all the different ideas I presented here. Yes, you can do it even if you are in a pleasant state mentally and emotionally. In fact, that is even better as you'll be able to observe more clearly how strongly these three aspects are interlinked.

If you are distressed in any way, then these techniques will definitely help you self-soothe. Go ahead and give them a try if you haven't tested them out yet. Come back to the rest of the chapter once you are done. Reading a book won't change your life but putting into practice what I am teaching you here will definitely have a massive positive impact on your life.

UNCONVENTIONAL BUT TRIED AND TESTED TECHNIQUES

A lot of my techniques may seem somewhat unconventional and different from what you would find professionals practicing. I am sharing these techniques with you because I have successfully used them to heal my own trauma. I use these methods and techniques to manage my emotions to this day. I won't share anything with you that I haven't tested out myself and that hasn't worked for me personally or for my clients.

Life is all about trial and error. To keep growing and evolving into the highest version of yourself, you have to test out different things. Some may work for you and some may not. Pick the ones that work for you and adopt them into your daily life. Always remember that you are the only one who knows what works best for you.

After using each technique, ask yourself, "How am I feeling?" Check to see if there has been any positive effect for you. You don't need to intellectually understand everything. In fact, trying to intellectualize everything can easily turn into a trap that never allows you to make any real progress. Instead, focus on and trust your own experience. Experiential learning is the best type of learning – only what you experience for yourself can be truly real for you.

THOUGHTS OCCUR IN LOOPS AND STEM FROM BELIEFS

When you are feeling overwhelmed by thoughts, it seems like there are too many of them to deal with. If instead of allowing them to loosely flow around in your mind, you'd take the time to sit down and write them, you'll discover something different. You'll realize that there aren't really that many thoughts plaguing and overwhelming you. Instead, it is some thoughts that get repeated over and over again.

Most likely, what you were thinking yesterday is what you are thinking today. What you are thinking today is what you'll be thinking tomorrow and so on. To change your thoughts, you have to intentionally choose differently. Since thoughts occur in loops, working on some thoughts that appear repeatedly will completely transform your thinking experience.

I am sure you have heard the saying that the mind is a wonderful servant but a terrible master. If you'll allow your untamed thoughts to run your life and guide your actions, you'll never achieve anything worthwhile. An untamed mind is like a garden that hasn't been tended to. You can't expect to experience beauty in such a garden. Weeds grow there and unpleasantness resides there. Your mind is your private garden. It depends entirely upon you to tend to it like a beautiful garden or leave it untended to.

You must also realize that your thoughts are your perceptions – they are your ideas of how things are or how they may be. They are not always rooted in reality. The vast majority of our thoughts stem from our belief system – what we believe to be true about the world, about ourselves, about our future, etc.

To transform your thoughts, you have to also work on your beliefs. The problem is that most people never sit down to question their beliefs – they take them for granted as if they were an objective reality true for everyone. What you believe in is what you think about. What you think about is what you experience in your reality.

Most of your beliefs are not even your own. They have been given to you by society, parents, teachers, and other people who played an influential role when you were growing up. These beliefs are reflections of what other people believed to be true for themselves and not what is actually true for you. For instance, maybe you were told, "You are so bad at math." At some point, you started believing in this statement. Once you start believing that something is impossible to achieve, you'll never put in the effort to improve yourself in that area.

If you believe you are bad at math, then espousing that belief immediately implies you'll consciously and subconsciously reject all possibilities of improving yourself at it. You are bad at math is someone else's idea that you accepted as your own belief. No matter what anyone else says, math is a skill that can be learned. You can teach yourself to be good at it but for that, you'll have to drop your limiting belief. You'll have to intentionally relinquish the idea that you are bad at math.

To transform your belief at the core level, you'll have to prop up a new belief by espousing new thoughts. This could mean repeating affirmations throughout the day and using positive self-talk. For our example, the affirmation can be, "I am brilliant at math!" Whenever you start feeling doubts and fears creep up, use positive self-talk like, "I know I can do this!" "I have the ability and the power to do this." "I am committed – getting better and improving every day is my only choice!"

EXERCISE

Write down all the thoughts that are on your mind right now. I would highly recommend writing with a pen in a journal. Typing is also okay. It's just that I have found writing with an actual pen on a physical paper compels us to be more present with our thoughts. You can do either but I would recommend physically writing things down if that's possible for you.

For the next three days, I want you to carry this journal with you everywhere you go. Whenever you start feeling overwhelmed, write down your thoughts. The simple act of writing everything down will help you feel lighter and less overwhelmed.

The process of writing also helps you distance yourself from your thoughts. Always remember that you are not your thoughts. Your thoughts are a part of you but they are not you. You don't have to judge yourself over the undesirable thoughts you get. Let them rise and fall like waves in an ocean.

Writing your thoughts down helps you look at them more objectively. You gain a different perspective when you read what you have written down. Also, the process of writing disperses a lot of the emotional charge that are associated with those thoughts. Journaling is, therefore, an excellent tool for managing and releasing difficult emotions.

By reading and evaluating what you have written down, you gain a fresh perspective. This helps you understand the direction in which you and your life are going. When you understand that, then you can direct the sails of your thoughts, emotions, and actions in your desired direction.

EVALUATE YOUR THOUGHTS

At the end of the three day period, it is time to process and evaluate your thoughts.

Read through everything and answer the following questions.

What are the recurring themes – thought patterns that are being repeated over and over again. For example; worries about finances, fear of marriage breaking down, etc. Try to identify the theme behind the frequently recurring thought patterns.

_____

_____

_____

_____

_____

_____

What is the one recurring theme that is bothering you the most right now? Pick the one that is weighing on you the heaviest resolving which will give you the greatest relief for now.

_____

_____

_____

_____

What are the negative thoughts associated with this theme? For instance, if you theme is financial worries, your thoughts can be something like this: I am never going to make enough money, I am afraid of losing money, etc.

_____

_____

_____

_____

_____

_____

_____

_____

What evidence do you have to support the legitimacy of these negative thoughts? Next to each negative thought write down the evidence you have to support its legitimacy. If there is no evidence or reason why you should believe that thought, then write down "no evidence." Feel free to use another sheet of paper if you run out of space here.

Evaluate the list you created. How many of your thoughts are legitimate in the sense that there is concrete evidence that you should believe these negative thoughts as truths? I am sure very few of those thoughts can be justified. Negative thoughts rooted in fear and anxiety arise from the limbic system which is associated with the fight or flight response.

We can't think rationally when fear takes over as even the smallest of threats is perceived as a life-or-death situation.

The good news is that you can train yourself to calm down and see the negative thoughts for what they really are – mostly irrational fears and illogical anxiety-inducing ideas. Note down the total number of thoughts that are completely irrational as in there is no evidence or legitimate reason why you should believe them as truths.

Now, go back and evaluate those thoughts that are justified in some way. For instance, maybe there is a 50% chance what you are afraid of can turn out to be true. Let me give you an example. Let us say your friend hasn't phoned you in a month. You fear they have severed all contact with you. There is a 50% chance that this can be true. But isn't there a 50% chance that they just got busy and life took over. Maybe they just haven't had a chance to get back to you because of how intense things got in their own life.

What is much healthier and better for you to believe? Choose the thoughts that are best for you and that serve your highest good. Another thing I'll tell you here is something I learned from a mentor of mine. He taught me an important lesson, "Never believe anything as the truth until you have concrete evidence to support its veracity." If you don't have concrete evidence to support your fear that your friend is intentionally ignoring you, then isn't it better to believe that they just got busy or have something going on in their own life which has nothing to do with you?

Write down those thoughts that are justified in some way, and then assess what is best for you to believe in.

EMOTIONS AND BEHAVIOR OCCUR IN PATTERNS

Just like how thoughts occur in loops, emotions and behavior occur in patterns. Think of that time when you thought, "Why do I keep doing this? I don't understand why I can't stop?" We do certain things because they have become established patterns for us. The same goes for emotions. We feel the same kind of emotions frequently and repeatedly because they have become part of our emotional patterns.

This is also the reason why so many people jump from one relationship to another. The face and name may change but the relationship they have with the other person remains the same. They find themselves acting in the same way feeling the same kind of emotions that they felt in the previous relationship. This is because we are constantly attracting people, situations, and circumstances that are aligned with our beliefs about the world.

You may think that the other person is the problem but if you keep experiencing the same thing over and over with different people, then you have to look at the common denominator in all those connections – you! I know how hard this is but you have to step into your power by taking 100% responsibility for your life. Taking responsibility doesn't mean condoning other people's bad behavior and feeling guilty or blaming yourself.

On the contrary, taking responsibility is all about claiming your power in every situation. You don't have control over how other people act but you have full control over your own actions. When you focus on what you can control in any situation, you feel powerful. When you blame others, you give your power away. This is not about who is right or who is wrong. It is about choosing what helps you feel powerful and moves you closer to your goals.

Your feelings, emotions, and thoughts influence your actions. For instance, if you aren't feeling confident and good about yourself, you'll act in ways that will confirm your negative beliefs about yourself. On the other hand, if you can get yourself to feel confident and content with who you are, you'll act in ways that will confirm your positive beliefs about yourself.

As I said earlier, thoughts, emotions, and behavior are strongly interlinked. You can influence your behavior by transforming how you feel about yourself but you can also influence how you feel about yourself by intentionally changing your actions. For instance, you can do things that will help your self-confidence. Whenever you start feeling bad about yourself, you can reference those times when you achieved something significant that boosted your confidence, it will help you in the present as well.

EXERCISE

For the next three days, carry a journal with you. Note down your thoughts at regular intervals but this time focus more on how you are feeling. Do this exercise every couple of hours – like at regular intervals of 2-3 hours. Do it when you are feeling good, when you are feeling neutral, when you are feeling negative, and everything in between. You want to accumulate enough data to analyze your emotional state.

Every time you create an entry focus on asking the following questions:

- What am I feeling right now?
- Where exactly in my body am I feeling these emotions?
- What is the behavior that these emotions are prompting you to engage in?

At the end of the three-day period, analyze the data you have collected and record your answers to the following questions.

What are the predominant emotions that you feel throughout the day? Like, anger, hatred, happiness, joy, etc.

Which one emotion do you experience most often? How does it make you feel? Like, if it is anger does it make you bitter, resentful, judgmental, critical, etc.?

Where exactly in your body do you feel this emotion?

What kind of action/s does this emotion prompt you to take?

Do you like the action/s you have been taking or are feeling tempted to take? Write down your reason explaining why you like or don't like the action/s you feel compelled to take.

If you don't like the action/s you have been taking, what can
you do to change? For instance, perhaps you can spend some
time with this emotion and decide to not do anything in the
heat of the moment. Give yourself a few hours to allow your
emotional state to calm down before taking any action.

By completing these exercises you'll realize just how strongly
linked your thoughts, emotions, and behavior are. Always

remember that self-awareness is the master key to trans-formation.

Be sure to complete all these exercises before moving on to the next chapter where we will discuss the two main coping strategies that everyone uses for processing their thoughts and emotions.

2

THE ROLE OF TRAUMAS AND
BELIEFS

"Your beliefs... your thoughts... your emotions... shape your life. Like magnets, they function to manifest occurrences in a chosen reality. What you most believe comes into your Life."

— ELLE NICOLAI

If you find yourself obsessively thinking about everything that can possibly go wrong and/or you often suffer from negative moods, the answer lies in your childhood. The blueprint for how we are going to experience life gets established pretty early on in childhood. To improve our adult relationships, whether with others or with our own self, we have to go back to the first relationship we formed with our primary caregivers.

I realized this fact a long time ago. For years, I struggled with dysfunctional relationships. I'll meet someone wonderful. Things would start out on a high note. The other person will be extremely invested in me. I would become convinced I have finally met the person I have been waiting for my whole life. Just when things would become extremely intense, the other person would back out a little. From that point on, things would get progressively worse. The harder I would try to salvage the relationship, the faster it would disintegrate.

I thought I was doomed or maybe cursed. It made no sense why I kept experiencing the same relationship pattern over and over again with different people. I started wondering if there was something wrong with me that made me undesirable when someone got too close to me. I also wondered if it was destiny to remain single and because of that none of the relationships ever worked out.

One day while casually browsing the psychology section of my favorite bookstore, I stumbled upon a book on attachment theory which was formulated by a psychiatrist called John Bowlby (Wikipedia, n.d.). I opened the book and read a few pages. What I read left my mouth agape – I had read a description of my own relationship pattern described with painful accuracy within the pages of the book. The more I learned about attachment theory, the clearer it became to me why my adult relationships were dysfunctional. It didn't have much to do with the present but had everything to do with my extremely challenging childhood.

I was the fourth child of my parents. Apparently, I was "a mistake" – I spent my entire childhood feeling like I didn't matter. My parents were very poor – they struggled to make ends meet. There was constant fighting and bickering over money. I am not entirely sure why they married each other because there was certainly no love in their relationship. My father was also openly cheating on my mother. My mother lacked the courage to walk out of the relationship. Even though she was making a living of her own, she felt psychologically and emotionally dependent upon her marriage.

Due to her own struggles and challenges, my mother was often in a bad mood. I felt unwanted and invisible. If I ever asked for something, she would blow up and make me feel guilty that I asked for anything at all. The idea that I was all alone became deeply embedded in my mind. I decided that if I ever wanted anything, I'd have to figure out how to get it on my own. I was just not one of those lucky children whose parents look after their every need. I felt deeply and profoundly alone in this world.

Even though I was the youngest child, I often took care of my older siblings. I would compromise with my own needs to cater to the needs of others because deep within, I felt that my own needs don't matter. As I described earlier, my mother had an explosive temper. I was scared of her unpredictable moods. She would blow up anytime, anywhere without even the slightest provocation.

The environment at home was so depressing that my heart used to sink at the idea of returning back home after school. For me, home was a place of pain, misery, dissatisfaction, disappointment, and dysfunction. I often dreamed of a happy family life. I would think to myself – one day I'll get married have my own family and every day of my life would be joyful.

Later on, as I studied attachment theory and learned about the damages that emotionally immature parents cause to their children, I realized that my dream of a happy family life was actually a "healing fantasy." Having the fantasy of a perfect life helped me cope with all the chaos and unhappiness that characterized my home life.

Later on, as I got older and started dating, I was very quick to fall in love and get attached. Only after I learned more about attachment styles and the concept of a healing fantasy that I realized all my life I had been looking for someone to give me the childhood I never had. I was so desperate to have the happy idyllic family life that I ignored all the red flags when I picked people who were damaged and wounded.

Indeed, not working through and healing our wounds make us vulnerable to forming relationships with other damaged and wounded people. In our society, instant chemistry – the type that sends chills down your spine and makes you obsessed with another person – is often glorified. Many people get married believing that life with their lover would be like a gondola ride through the glorious canals of Venice. Instead, a little while later, they realize the other person is just as imperfect as everyone else. Being with someone does require work. It also requires radical unconditional acceptance of oneself and one's partner.

When old wounds come to the surface to be healed in intimate relationships, people think they have fallen out of love with the other person. They don't want to do the work of looking within and healing the wounds that have been triggered and brought to the surface by the presence of their partner. Instead, they erroneously place the blame for their pain on their partner and hop from one relationship to another searching for that one perfect person who will "save" them.

I was waiting to be saved and every time someone showed me the possibility of having a happy family life and then disappeared from my life, I felt depressed and dejected. Once I started understanding my attachment style, it became clear to me that my experiences in the present were rooted in the past. I had to go back to my childhood and start healing my extreme fear of abandonment. I had felt abandoned by my family – I was waiting to be saved by someone who could give me the childhood I never had.

Due to my extreme fear of abandonment, I was perpetually in a hyper-vigilant stage – looking for signs that the other person is going to leave me. I'd remain at the edge of my seat waiting for the last show to drop. It became a self-fulfilling prophecy. Through my intimate relationships, I was getting to relive and re-experience the feeling of being abandoned that had characterized my early childhood experiences.

Interestingly enough, I was constantly attracting and being attracted to partners who were anxious avoidant – individuals who had also been damaged in their childhood. Instead of becoming anxious preoccupied, they became anxious avoidant. The former makes a person obsessed with seeking intimacy with other people while the latter revolve around a deep fear of experiencing authentic intimacy with another person.

I am sharing this story with you to help you understand how our beliefs, thoughts, and behavior patterns get shaped by our early childhood experiences. Most of the things we believe to be true are not our own beliefs but what we picked up from the belief system of our primary caregivers. The thoughts we think frequently stem from our belief system. We can transform our behavior patterns in the present only by healing our childhood traumas. We must go back in time and transform the beliefs, ideas, and thoughts we picked up from our primary caregivers that don't serve our highest good.

The good news is that we are highly programmable beings. The ignorance of our caregivers programmed us in the wrong way. I am not suggesting that we should be angry or bitter toward them. Keep in mind, they did the best that they were capable of based on the knowledge and understanding they had. It is likely that their caregivers didn't treat them any better so how they treated us was just a result of what they had learned from those who came before them.

No matter what you have experienced, blaming others should not be an option. Not because you should condone other people's wrong actions but because the moment you put the blame on someone else, you give the power away. If someone else is responsible for how you are feeling and living your life, you hand over your power to them. Instead, you can take 100% responsibility for who you are and how you feel. By doing this, you instantly become more powerful. When you ask yourself what you can do now to create the life you want and to be the highest version of yourself, you reclaim your power.

Once I realized that my early childhood had given me an anxious preoccupied attachment style, I was able to ask myself the question, "How can I heal myself and turn this negative into a positive?" Indeed, life is all about turning our weaknesses into strengths. Your greatest challenges are your greatest opportunities for growth. My early childhood experience didn't automatically provide me with a secure attachment style that could support healthy adult relationships but it was in my hands to develop a secure attached style. I learned self-soothing techniques and methods to calm myself when bouts of anxiety would engulf me. Don't worry,

I'll share some of the best techniques with you in this book as well. Learning to self-soothe is absolutely essential for emotional regulation.

Over time, with tremendous self-awareness and an unwavering commitment to healing my inner child, I developed a secure attachment style. There are days when bouts of anxiety become to resurface but now, I have the knowledge to manage it appropriately. I have been married for a long time now to a partner who also has a secure attachment style. In life, at any point of time, you can become whoever you want to be.

Turning your life around is entirely in your own hands. The question is are you fully committed to changing your life? If the answer is yes, then continue reading on. You are on your way to an incredibly exciting and rewarding life. If the answer is no, then, sit back and take your time to reflect – what is it that's holding you back from taking full responsibility and committing to turn all your dreams into reality?

EXERCISE

Take a few moments to close your eyes and think about a traumatic experience from your childhood. Some people become triggered by the mere suggestion that there can be traumatic experiences in their childhood. Pretty much everyone in this world has suffered some kind of trauma or another. If you are struggling to recall such an experience, then just relax by breathing deeply. Let your mind take you to whatever negative experience comes up first irrespective of the age you were at.

It is going to be hard but allow yourself to fully relive that experience. Write down your thought and feelings about that experience in as much detail as possible. If you run out of space here, then use a separate sheet to continue writing down your thoughts and feelings. Write for as long as you need to. After pouring everything down on paper, you'll feel lighter, especially if you have never shared the details about this incident with anyone yet.

_____

_____

_____

_____

_____

_____

_____

_____

_____

_____

How has this incident impacted your life? What changed in you and your life after this incident?

Do you like who you have become because of this incident? I would urge you to not think of things as black and white. The beauty of life lies in its complexity. There are many shades of grey. While the incident may have had a negative impact on you, there is also a chance that it has contributed to your growth and evolution. If the latter isn't true yet, then that is how you can use this incident to create a better life for yourself and become a more evolved version of yourself.

_____

_____

_____

_____

_____

_____

_____

_____

_____

_____

_____

_____

Write an apology letter to your younger self expressing how sorry you are that you allowed your inner child to suffer so much (Your inner child lives inside you no matter how many candles you have had on your birthday cake). Tell your inner child that you are deeply sorry that you couldn't take a stand for yourself at that time but from now on, you'll always be there for yourself.

You are the only one who can save you. You must begin now by fully committing to standing by your own side no matter what. Whatever it is that you didn't receive from others, you have the power to give to yourself. You just need to decide that you are ready and willing to do whatever it takes to always be there for yourself.

In the letter, be sure to express all the love and care that you wish you had received from someone else at the time. Give it to yourself like you were your own best friend looking after yourself. You can use the space here to write the letter. If you run out of space, then feel free to use separate sheets to continue writing.

BELIEFS SHAPE OUR REALITY

Beliefs are the blueprint that shape our experience of reality. If you don't like anything in your reality, you can't change it by fighting the manifestation you are seeing in the outer world. Instead, you'll have to go inside and explore the beliefs that have birthed those experiences in the outer world. Think of it like this – if you were watching a movie in a movie theatre, you won't fight the projections on the screen. Instead, you'll change the reel that is being played.

To change the reel that is getting projected on the screen of your life, you'll have to work on your beliefs. I am not talking about what you believe to be true at the conscious level. Your conscious thoughts and ideas don't impact your reality to the extent that your subconscious beliefs do. Your beliefs are thoughts and ideas that you have accepted as truths. Many of them serve you and many don't. You have to identify the ones that are holding you back and replace them with new empowering beliefs that serve your highest good.

"This is how humans are: We question all our beliefs, except for the ones that we really believe in, and those we never think to question."

— ORSON SCOTT CARD

As this quote suggests pausing to question our deeply held beliefs is one of the hardest things in the world. We often mistake negative beliefs for facts. I'll share another story with you that will illustrate how this works.

When I was in second grade, I joined a singing class. One day our teacher asked each one of us to sign a few lines individually. When my turn came, I did my best but to my horror, everyone except the teacher laughed at me. I felt so embarrassed that I wished I could just disappear into the earth at that moment. The kids mocked me for being an awful singer. Interestingly enough, till that point, I had never thought I was a bad singer. But because of what I was told, I accepted the idea that I was an awful singer as a fact.

I never made any effort to improve my singing skills. After all, what was the point when I already knew I was an awful singer? I created this reality for myself where there was no possibility for ever becoming a better singer. The belief that I was a bad singer was handed over to me by society and I accepted it as my reality.

Many years passed and I never again dared to sing publicly. A few years back I became friends with someone who is a classical singer. She would often remark to me, "You have such a wonderful voice, you should try singing." I wasn't sure why she would think I had a voice fit for singing when could barely sing a line without subjecting myself to embarrassment and ridicule.

One day I agreed to accompany her to a singing workshop she was conducting for aspiring singers. I was really nervous to sing again publicly but this time, no one laughed at me. Instead, I received encouragement. I was told I have a good voice, and I just need to work on my rhythm and pitch. This feedback got me excited. I wanted to see if I could become good at something I had believed my entire life I was bad at.

I started learning the right techniques for singing. I practiced regularly. I am proud to say that at this stage of my life most people in my life think that I am an amazing singer. Teaching myself to sing was an exercise in breaking a belief system that was holding me back from realizing my full potential in life. I accepted someone else's opinion of me as a fact for what I can do and who I can be in this life. It was also an opportunity for me to heal the trauma of being mocked and shamed.

I may not have had inborn musical talent but that doesn't mean I was doomed to be a terrible singer my entire life. There are many things we can teach ourselves by sheer determination and force of will.

In the book Mindset, Carol Dweck explains the difference between a fixed mindset and a growth mindset. What we believe to be true about our talents and abilities has the strongest impact on our success or lack of it. People with a fixed mindset believe that we either have certain abilities or we don't. Those who have a growth mindset believe that abilities can be developed. It may not be easy but it is definitely possible! One of my favorite quotes from the book is, "It's not always the people who start out the smartest who end up the smartest." (Dweck, 2007)

I really want you to sit down and think about who you want to be in this life and how you want to live your life. This book is about regulating emotions but our emotions and thoughts don't occur in isolation. They are connected to who we are, what we believe to be true, and the goals that we set for ourselves. Most people drift through life without ever deciding clearly who they want to be and how they want to live their life.

When you know what kind of person you want to be, you'll also know what kind of thoughts and emotions would be associated with that person. Similarly, the ideal life you want to live would be supported by certain thoughts, emotions, and beliefs. Without a goal, you'll never be able to give a clear direction to your mind and heart.

Once you have identified your goals, you'll need to look at the thoughts, ideas, and beliefs that are holding you back from living your dream life. You'll have to transform them into thoughts, ideas, and beliefs that support you. The exercises I am going to share with you now will help you in this process. Be sure to complete all the exercises before moving on to the next chapter. Always remember that your life is not going to change by reading a book. It is going to change only when you are doing the work to transform your life.

EXERCISE

Write a description of your ideal self – don't hold yourself back. Think of it like making a Christmas wish. What would you write if I told you that whatever you are writing here will definitely come true? Trust me, it will! Everything is possible in this life.

_____

_____

_____

What kind of thoughts, beliefs, emotions, and ideas does this person have?

Write a description of your ideal life – how you want to live, what your daily life is like, how you spend your time, etc. Again, don't hold yourself back. Think of it like making a Christmas wish. What would you write if I told you that whatever you are writing here will definitely come true? Trust me, it will! Everything is possible in this life.

_____

_____

_____

_____

_____

_____

_____

_____

_____

_____

_____

What do you believe to be true right now that is preventing you from being your ideal self and living your ideal life? Is it really a belief or is it a fact? Next to each point, write down "B" for belief and "F" for a fact. For instance, you have two legs and two hands is a fact but you are terrible at math is a belief. The latter can be improved if you become committed to becoming great at math.

Most of the things we believe to be facts are actually strongly held beliefs. It is very hard to identify these beliefs. You just have to become skeptical about absolutely everything you have believed to be true so far. Some things may be a fact but even they can be changed. Like, you have brown hair may be a fact but if you don't like brown hair on yourself, then you can change it to another color you like better. Life provides us with infinite possibilities.

What practical actions can you take to turn your negative beliefs into facts? Pick one belief transforming which will have the greatest positive impact on your life right now, and then start working on it. For instance, going back to being bad at math example, you can commit to taking classes and practicing math problems daily. If you'll stick with anything long enough while doing your best to improve yourself by a marginal percentage every day constantly, a day will come when you'll become exceptional at it.

_____

_____

_____

_____

_____

_____

_____

_____

_____

_____

3

EVALUATE, DESIGN, AND OPTIMIZE YOUR EXTERNAL ENVIRONMENT

"You can't make positive choices for the rest of your life without an environment that makes those choices easy, natural, and enjoyable."

— DEEPAK CHOPRA

The influence of one's immediate environment can never be underestimated. Indeed, you can overcome the influence of one's environment to a very large extent but it is very hard to do it consistently, constantly, and for extended periods of time. It is akin to swimming against the tide – you can do it for a while but it begins to get really exhausting after some time.

Who we are, how we process emotions, and the thoughts we think regularly are all strongly linked to our external environment. Our external environment doesn't just comprise the physical surroundings in which we spend our days but also the people with whom we spend the vast majority of our time. By simply being around other people, we subconsciously adopt their habits, ways of thinking, and even their emotional responses.

If you surround yourself with confident and happy people, then after a while you will become like them as well. If you surround yourself with depressed and dejected people, then you will soon feel depleted. If you surround yourself with cynical and angry people, then it is only a matter of time before you'll internalize those negative qualities.

Many people get triggered by this idea. They don't want to believe that others are having such a powerful influence over them. Many people also find the idea that they are being influenced by others quite wounding to the ego. No matter how you perceive it, this is a fact of life. Who you surround yourself with determines your destiny to a great extent. Therefore, it only makes sense that positive transformation should not be limited to making changes in one's inner world. It is absolutely imperative to extend those efforts to one's external environment as well.

Honestly, I used to be one of those people who thought the environment cannot affect me. At that time, everyone in my surroundings was struggling financially. They all had a lot of limiting beliefs around money. Every time I made a little progress, I would regress back to the same level as everyone else. I was tired of living paycheck to paycheck never having enough money to live the kind of life I had always wanted to live.

One day I attended a workshop where the coach asked all of us to write down the names of the people with whom we were spending the maximum amount of our time. Later on, our coach asked us to also write down the income of each person. If we didn't know the exact amount, we could write an approximate amount.

We were asked to write down the average of everyone's income and evaluate how close our own income was to the average. Shockingly enough, my income was almost exactly at the same level as the average income of my peer group. That day I learned the most important lesson of my life. Environment often trumps willpower. I was trying hard to get out of my financial struggles but the lack of positive role models in my immediate environment was preventing me from moving forward.

As human beings, we are also strongly impacted by the mindset and attitude of the people around us. At the subconscious level, we begin to mirror the people we are constantly surrounded by. Every person has a mental model that dictates their experience of life. A person's mental model is composed of a set of ideas and beliefs that dictate their experiences through life. If you are surrounded by people who have the same challenges as you, then it will be very hard for you to overcome them.

You need to expose yourself to people who have the results you want and those who have successfully overcome the challenges you are facing. It can also be beneficial to have people around you who are in the process of overcoming the challenges you are also working on. This way you can learn from their experiences as well but if you are only surrounded by people who have no interest in overcoming those challenges, then it will be very hard for you to get positive results.

Jim Rohn famously said, "You are the average of the five people you spend the most time with." (Rohn, n.d.) I can't emphasize enough how true this is! No matter how strong your willpower is, you will inevitably get influenced by the people around you. If the people you are spending all your time with have no emotional control, then you will also struggle to manage your emotions. Once I changed my company, my life transformed rapidly.

I deliberately started surrounding myself with people who were successful and wealthy. Initially, it wasn't easy so I was spending most of my time alone. I started reading books, listening to podcasts, and watching videos featuring successful people. Over time, their mindset and attitude toward life started rubbing off on me. I also realized that successful and wealthy people have a completely different mental model of the world than those who are financially struggling. As I continued on my path of self-improvement, I started meeting people who were massively successful. Eventually, as I kept making progress, my peer group transformed completely.

No matter what your goals are, you MUST surround yourself with people who have achieved what you want to achieve. If you can't get access to them in person right now, then fret not! We are living in one of the greatest eras that humanity has witnessed. You can be in the company of the most successful people in the world with just a few clicks. Read books written by these people, listen to their podcasts, watch their interviews, and capitalize on any opportunity you can find to learn from them. By simply putting yourself in their vicinity, you'll begin to make progress.

Over time, you'll start attracting such people into your life, and as you walk continue moving forward on your own journey of self-improvement. Don't underestimate the power of the company you keep. It is truly a game changer and one of the most important things you must master in life if you want to live a fulfilling life. How each person defines success can differ from individual to individual. But the idea of success modeling remains true for everyone. To become successful at anything, you need role models who have already achieved what you want to achieve. By observing them, learning from them, and modeling your own habits and actions after theirs, you can also achieve the success they have.

EXERCISE

What are your greatest struggles right now? Feel free to list them all, and then pick one to work on for now. It should be something that improving it will have the greatest positive impact on your life. For instance, let us say this was my list: poor financial situation, poor physical health, anger issues, sadness, and despondency.

Now, if I analyze this list, it is obvious to me that poor health is impacting all areas of life. Working on improving physical health will have a positive impact on all areas of life. Use this strategy to determine which area is most urgently in need of transformation right now and then start working on it. As you make progress and get results, pick one more item from the list and work on overcoming that challenge as well. Repeat this process until you have ticked off every single item of your list.

Name five people with whom you are spending the vast majority of your time. Do they have the same struggle as the one you have just committed to overcoming? Write down a "yes" or a "no" next to each person's name.

If the answer is "yes," then it would be in your best interest to figure out how you can limit your time around them. In a lot of cases, it may be difficult to not remain in physical proximity to that person. You can work on establishing strong boundaries with them. Tell them what you are willing to talk to about them and which topics you would rather avoid.

Avoid discussing your struggles with them when they have the same ones and they aren't committed to overcoming those struggles. If you can really limit the amount of time you spend with them, then that would be the best strategy. Like, you could totally disconnect or limit seeing them to a few special days a year. When you do meet them, stick to pleasant neutral topics that don't require deep conversations.

If the answer is "no," then you can use them as a positive role model and learn from them. Ask them if they have ever faced the challenge that you are facing and how they overcame it. Observe what kind of habits and attitudes they have that you can also cultivate. Try to observe them keenly and learn as much from them as possible. Focus on what they are doing differently that you can also apply to your life and then test it out.

Name five people who have the kind of results you want for yourself. Next to each person's name write down how you can bring yourself in their proximity and learn from them. Like, if it is someone you know in person, you can invite them to play golf together or capitalize on any other common interest you both have. Always seek to add value by learning what you can do for them instead of trying to use others for your own benefit.

If it is a famous person you admire, then make note of all the resources through which you can learn more about them. Like, by reading their books, listening to their interviews, etc. Pay attention to how they are living their life not only vis-à-vis the primary area of focus you have right now but in all areas of life. Of course, no one is an expert at everything.

You have to use your discretion to decide what you want to learn from someone and where it is not worth listening to them. Different people have different expertise. The secret to learning effectively from everyone is to always have your filter on. The most successful people in the world have powerful filters in place through which they sift all information to decide what's useful and what's not.

THE ROLE OF YOUR PHYSICAL ENVIRONMENT

I was struggling to complete an important project while working from home. My colleague was on the phone asking me what was going on – why was I lagging behind on the deadline? Out of sheer frustration, this colleague asked me, "Tell me, what does your environment look like right now?"

I was stunned for a few moments and then I felt ashamed. I sheepishly admitted, "It's messy." He balked and said, "That's exactly what is wrong. You can't be productive while being surrounded by so much clutter." After that, he said a line that has stayed with me my entire life, "Your physical space is a reflection of your mental space." How profound was that! Yet, until that point, I had never thought about the role that my physical environment was playing in my overall productivity and mood.

I didn't learn the lesson right away. The idea was so novel and rather strange to me that it took me a long time to truly begin to understand how strongly we are impacted by the physical environment we live in. My colleague had planted a seed in my mind. I started exploring this new idea – the correlation between one's mental environment and immediate physical space. I started observing how these two correlate for other people and not just for me.

I immediately started seeing patterns. People who were disorganized in their thoughts and lacked clarity almost always have chaotic physical environments. I also observed that every time my physical environment became too overwhelming for me that I had to begin decluttering, I felt mentally and energetically lighter. Many a time, it felt as if a heavy weight had been lifted off my shoulders.

Similarly, every time, I did some inner decluttering by mentally, emotionally, and spiritually letting go of that which wasn't serving me, I also felt a powerful urge to declutter my physical space. It is really fascinating how the inner and the outer world correlate. It is almost impossible to not have the transformation replicated in both worlds to some degree at least when one is working on either of the two aspects.

For me, this was truly a life changing revelation. I could never go back to being as messy as I used to be. Once I read Marie Kondo's *The Life-Changing Magic of Tidying Up*, it became even clearer to me that what I had learned was true and very real – our physical environment has a powerful impact upon our inner world and vice versa.

So now let me ask you this question. Put this book down for a moment and spend some time looking around. What do you see? Is your space organized, neat, and tidy? Is it messy, chaotic, and dirty? Your environment affects your moods and mental state to a much larger degree than you realize. When you are living with someone else, it becomes quite hard to have things your way but still you can try to organize and tidy your personal spaces as best as possible.

"You are a product of your environment. So choose the environment that will best develop you toward your objective. Analyze your life in terms of its environment. Are the things

around you helping you toward success - or are they holding
you back?"

— W. CLEMENT STONE

Emotional regulation has a lot to do with the physical environment we spend the vast majority of our time in. There are places that energize us and there are places that deplete us. I am sure you have experienced this before – you enter a room or a house and you suddenly start feeling drained. Even if you can't point your finger at exactly what it is, something about that environment makes you feel ill at ease. Similarly, some places have a refreshing and rejuvenating effect on us. They leave us feeling energized and vivacious.

The good news is that you can intentionally organize your environment in a way that brings you joy and peace. Colors, prints, designs, and how things are placed around a physical space all have their own unique effect on us. I would suggest that you explore and learn more about all these different aspects. I am suggesting that you need to completely redo your physical space. Such a feat may or may not be within your budget right now.

But it doesn't cost anything extra to let go of all those items that are no longer serving you and intentionally surround yourself only with those items that support the kind of life you want to live and the person that you want to be. I would highly recommend that you read Marie Kondo's *The Life-Changing Magic of Tidying Up* to learn more about decluttering.

In a lot of ways bringing order to your physical environment is the act of confronting yourself. In order to let go of things that no longer serve you or evoke any positive feelings in you, you are also getting to know yourself better. You become compelled to face things that you may not have dealt with before. Like, a gift given by an old flame may be negatively impacting your mood than adding value to your life at this point in time. Perhaps there is that tea set you inherited from your late aunt that you find really ugly but are struggling to get rid of because of its sentimental value and because you feel you'll be betraying your late aunt by giving it away. Marie addresses all these issues very tactfully in her book.

It is best to let go of items that feel more like an obligation than something you truly value and want to have around you. It is also worth exploring utilizing it for alternate purposes instead of trying to use them only for their original intended purpose. By clearing and rearranging your environment, you'll immediately make it easier for yourself to be in a pleasant mood every day. Of course, no one is ever happy 24/7 but you can optimize your environment to support positive emotions.

The act of putting your environment in order is also very useful when you are feeling ill at ease and distressed in some way. It is excellent for channelizing your energy and helping you put your energy to good use. When we are going through tough times, the natural instinct is to hide in bed and not get up at all. I am sure you have also done that at some point and it left you feeling even more dejected and drained.

In those times, having a routine really helps. I would not recommend tackling major decluttering projects during such times but stick to the routine tasks that you perform on a daily basis. Most people allow their routine to go completely haywire when things get really challenging, especially when faced with grief. During such times, sticking to a routine really helps. It provides a sense of groundedness and gives your energy a sense of direction when you are feeling like you are all over the place.

When you are struggling to bring peace and order to your internal environment, try putting your external environment in order first. The feeling you gain from it will translate into your inner world and you'll automatically start feeling more at ease with yourself.

EXERCISE

On a scale of 0 to 10 how cluttered is your environment (with 10 being extremely cluttered and 0 being not cluttered at all)? If your space is cluttered, then write down how it makes you feel. Do you feel overwhelmed by it, does it make you uneasy, etc.?

_____

_____

_____

_____

_____

_____

_____

_____

Are you satisfied with your physical environment? If no, then what can you do to improve your physical environment?

_____

_____

_____

_____

Are you holding on to items that you no longer like or need but you have to keep them because you spent money on them or because someone you cared about gave them to you? Note down the names of 5-10 such items. How does it feel to have such items around? Do they evoke positive feelings in you or they are a source of negative energy that leaves you feeling uneasy?

When it comes to these items that don't serve you any more can you give them away or put them to alternative use? Note down who you can give them to or how you can use them for alternative purposes.

Spend 10 minutes decluttering your space. You can pick a corner and declutter only that space. Get rid of 2 things you don't use anymore. Write down here how you felt after doing this exercise. Complete this exercise before moving on to the next section. You won't realize just how powerful it is until you try it out for yourself.

Note down all the feelings that came up for you during the process and after you completed the task. If you felt great,

268 | S. S. LEIGH

then add 10 minutes of decluttering to your daily schedule. It is one of the most effective ways of keeping your space in order and also an act of confronting your inner self through the medium of your external environment.

On a scale of 0-10, rate how clean your space is with 10 being extremely clean and 0 being extremely dirty. If you are not satisfied with the cleanliness of your space, then write down how you can improve the situation. Look into systems and methods that will help you create an easy-to-follow cleaning routine. If possible, you can also consider hiring help and paying someone else for it.

If cleaning is something you struggle with, then I would highly recommend reading the book *A Monk's Guide to a Clean House and Mind* by Shoukei Matsumoto. It is an extremely powerful book that may help transform your attitude and outlook towards cleaning. Maintaining a clean physical space is extremely important for maintaining internal hygiene. When you keep your space clean, you also polish your thoughts and emotions.

4

MASTERING YOUR INNER WORLD

"Take charge of your inner world by destroying the limitations caused by the outer distractions."

— HIRAL NAGDA

Your inner world creates and maintains the blueprint that dictates all your experiences in the outer world. Think about this – when you are in a good mood, it seems as if the entire world is joyful and happy. On the other hand, when you are in a bad mood, it seems as if every person you meet is grumpy and grouchy. Somehow the world outside has the ability to mirror our inner world to an unprecedented level of accuracy.

In the last chapter, I talked about intentionally organizing and optimizing your environment to support the kind of life you want to live. I covered the topic of working on your external environment first because making changes on the outside is often a lot easier than bringing about inner change.

Also, when you make changes in your external environment the results are concrete and clearly visible. Changes in the internal environment are often a lot more subtle and can often be hard to decipher. For instance, you don't always know the level of mental fortitude you have or that you have developed until you come-to-face with an extremely challenging situation and successfully overcome it.

While changes in the external environment are crucial for creating a congenial and harmonious atmosphere for our true self to thrive, it is through inner transformation that you will reach your highest potential in life. Your thoughts and emotions are part of your inner world. The outer world impacts it to a certain extent but without the right attitude, even the most harmonious outer atmosphere won't help you grow and reach your highest potential.

If you don't like your results in the external world, then you have to dive deep into your inner world. This book is called Emotional Regulation Skills but your thoughts and emotions are not problems to be dealt with. To thrive in life, you must get rid of the idea that certain thoughts or emotions are problematic. My goal with this book is not to teach you how to shut down those parts of yourself that society and other people have told you are undesirable.

There was a time in my life when I used to think the same way – that I need to shut down all "negative" thinking and constantly be in an elated happy mood. Life doesn't work like that. As humans, we are here to experience the full spectrum of what it means to be truly human. No emotion or thought is undesirable. Every emotion and every thought arises from a part of us that is seeking to be heard. We have to acknowledge all parts of us instead of trying to embrace only those parts that we believe are undesirable and abandon the ones we think are undesirable.

Through this book, I want to help you embrace yourself fully. The goal is not just to master your emotions and conquer your thoughts but to gain mastery over yourself. You automatically master your thoughts and emotions when you master yourself as they are parts of you. You must never treat them as separate from your Self. When you apply approaches to embrace and master all aspects of your being, your life transforms so deeply and intensely that you'll be amazed by who you have become even in a relatively short amount of time.

GIVE UP JUDGMENT

Socrates famously said, "The unexamined life is not worth living." (Socrates, n.d.) Indeed, you have to understand and examine your life very closely in order to gain mastery over it and over yourself. Make note here – the keyword is "understanding." In order to truly understand you must give up all judgment.

For me, one of the most empowering things has been to realize that everyone in the world has the same struggles as me. Most of the things we struggle with are human struggles. So if the alarm bell goes off and you keep putting it on snooze, it isn't just you. When you finally wake up, you say to yourself, "I am such a loser. I can't even wake up on time."

When you think it is just you who has these struggles, you start assuming there is something wrong with you but there is not a single person on the planet who hasn't done this or thought the same thing at some point. Always keep in mind that we are only looking at an external visage that other people are showing us. It is a carefully curated image of how someone wants to be seen and what they are allowing others to see. You don't know what someone's internal struggles are.

It may seem like highly productive and materially successful people have everything figured out but there isn't a single person in the world who isn't struggling with something. You can only be highly functional – perfection is an illusion. The only thing that separates the go-getters from the rest is that the former have trained themselves to take action and do what needs to be done irrespective of how they are feeling or all the doubts and fears that are plaguing them.

Yes, there isn't a single person on this planet who doesn't have some kind of fear or doubt. You can never get rid of them completely. You can only train yourself to act in spite of them.

Self-acceptance is the key to self-love. Self-transformation is enabled only through radical self-love. You have to embrace all parts of yourself if you want to love yourself fully, and, hence, transform yourself to be the person you have always wanted to be. It's all in your own hands. A lot of the labels that you have given yourself are not your own perceptions. They are labels and ideas that other people put upon you. Our early childhood experience dictates how we show up in life as an adult.

If your caregivers told you, "You are not good at this or that." It is only an idea. It is their perception of you. You heard it so many times that you decided to accept it as your truth. Since you accepted something as your truth, it became a part of your identity. From now on, I want you to start questioning every limiting belief you have. If you find yourself saying things like, "I am such an idiot" "I can't get anything right" – pause for a moment if what you are saying is really the truth. What evidence do you have to prove that the label or judgment you are subjecting yourself to is actually true? What are the counterarguments that oppose this idea?

I always say that the most important quality a person needs to develop is self-awareness. You have to start looking deep into your soul and being to start understanding yourself.

Don't accept any idea that doesn't serve you – question it, dissect it, and eventually, you'll be ready to discard it. What doesn't serve you should not have any place in your life.

Curate your thoughts, your emotions, your attitudes, and your outlook like you were responsible for maintaining the most beautiful garden in the world. It's true anyway – paradise is within you and so is hell. We create our own private heaven or hell depending upon the thoughts and emotions we choose to hold on to. Knowing it's all a choice is an extremely empowering realization. If you have chosen something you don't like, then you also have the power to choose differently now.

EXERCISE

Complete the following sentences with whatever negative beliefs or ideas come up in your mind. Don't think too much – the response that comes up immediately is essentially your programming.

I am terrible at

I can never do

I am such a/an

I hate myself when

I feel stupid when

I doubt that I am/I would

I always mess up

I struggle with

I will never be good at

Now, I want you to take a separate sheet of paper and write down each statement on top of it. Divide the page into two columns – write down on top "evidence" and "counter-evidence." In the first column write down all the evidence you have that proves the statement is correct. In the second column, write down why the statement is incorrect. Think of all those times when you did something that proves the statement is incorrect. Note down all the logical reasons why the statement is totally unfounded. Do it for all the statements. By the end of this exercise, you'll be surprised by the results.

A lot of things that we allow ourselves to believe are at best extremely faulty arguments that aren't grounded in reality at all. Logically working through these statements by weighing the evidence against the counter-evidence exposes how shoddy these beliefs are. Most of them aren't your own at all but ideas and beliefs you acquired from other people while growing up. They aren't a reflection of who you are but of the limited understanding that the person who transmitted these ideas to you had.

They believed certain things to be true about this world and of themselves, they projected those beliefs onto you. For instance, if they believed they can't do something, they'd tell you it can't be done. At some point, you started believing their words because repetition has that kind of power. If anything is repeated often enough, the mind starts accepting it as the truth. This is also why affirmations are so effective.

We can break down negative programming by constantly repeating new empowering beliefs.

Also, I am sure you didn't find it hard to come up with sentences to complete each one of the phrases. Trust me, it isn't just you. Every single person can fill the above questionnaire with ease because there is no one in this world who isn't grappling with some kind of doubt, insecurity or limiting beliefs. In life, we never truly arrive. No matter how far we have come, there is always another level at which we can play the game of life which requires us to advance even further and become an even finer version of ourselves.

Challenges are an essential part of life. The only thing that changes as you grow and become more is the way you deal with these challenges. The things that used to debilitate you previously become easy to tackle. At the same time, you have newer opportunities for growth in the form of new challenges you must overcome. There are infinite levels at which the game of life can be played. You can either look at it as something tragic or rejoice in the realization that the process of life is immensely dynamic and the opportunities for growth within just one human life are infinite.

YOUR THOUGHTS REVEAL A LOT ABOUT YOUR INNER AND OUTER WORLD

Your thoughts are like waves of an ocean – they arise and subside of their own accord. Don't try to hold on to them too tightly by dissecting and analyzing them. It will only frustrate and annoy you. Instead, your focus should be on witnessing them. Hold on to the ones that serve you and let go of the ones that aren't aligned with your highest good.

Our thoughts are strongly influenced by our external environment and by the company we keep. At the same time, our external environment and the company we are keeping are reflections of our internal framework that was established while growing up.

For instance, if you grew up in a highly dysfunctional family where your needs were hardly ever acknowledged and met, you may have anger issues and other emotional/behavioral problems. You'll attract people who are similar to you and you will constantly find yourself in environments that are aligned with the beliefs you have about the world.

So let us say you believe the world is full of jerks. You will constantly find yourself in the company of jerks. In life, we can never have more than what we believe we deserve. If you believe that living in a ramshackle house is all you deserve, then you simply won't be able to get yourself to be in a beautiful and luxurious house. Our beliefs and internal frameworks dictate every single experience of life.

At the same time, once you realize how the faulty programming of your internal world is holding you back and you start taking substantial steps to transform your reality, the people who are in your immediate environment won't like it at all. They will judge you, say harsh things to you, and will try to hold you back. It's not like they are bad people.

Most people aren't really thinking about their actions – they just act. And the reason why people engage in this kind of behavior is because you making improvements to your life often makes others uncomfortable. It holds a mirror to them and since they are not ready to make those same kinds of changes for whatever reason, they will be harsh and critical towards you in other to discourage you.

This is why you must constantly re-evaluate and reassess whether your peer group is holding you back in life or it is helping you make substantial progress in the direction of your goals. If you are constantly surrounded by pessimistic and negative people, then you will also become afflicted by such thoughts. It is also possible that your peer group may have served you at one point but that same group isn't aligned with who you are right now.

Most people are not growing and leveling up in life. If growth and being the highest version of yourself are priorities for you, then you must be willing to let go of people who are not aligned with who you are and where you want to go. Trust that nature abhors a vacuum. You will definitely meet new people who are better aligned with who you are and where you want to go.

I know I talked at length about the importance of surrounding yourself with the right people in the previous chapter but this topic is so important that I couldn't help reiterating it here as well. The other aspect that we must look at is that your thoughts arise from different parts of you. There are parts of you that "nurture" you and there are those parts of you that "protect" you. They are like your internal mother and father.

The aspect of you that is a protector has internalized the voice of the primary caregiver who was most critical of you. This voice chides you and is constantly cautioning you not to do certain things. Whenever you have a negative experience that causes you pain, it gets stored in your subconscious mind. If you encounter a similar situation in the future, the protector warns you again. For instance, if you had several failed relationships and you meet a new person with whom you are exploring the possibility of exploring a new relationship, the protector may constantly be on guard waiting for things to go wrong because that's what happened last time.

The protector may also caution you against trusting this new person and may try to talk you out of forging a relationship with them. Instead of rejecting the protector, you must acknowledge all the "negative" thoughts and understand that they come from a part of you which is seeking to be heard. All parts of you want the best for you. The nurturer encourages you and helps you move forward while the protector tries its best to prevent the recurrence of painful experiences from the past.

Your goal is to strengthen the voice of the nurturer while also hearing and acknowledging the protector. Let the protector know that you understand their intentions, acknowledge their concerns, and appreciate what they are doing for you. Once you do this, you'll feel immediate relief. Those "negative" thoughts that were bothering you so much would cease to have so much power and influence over you.

Pain comes from rejection. When you don't hear and acknowledge all aspects of yourself, those parts would scream louder for your attention. Give up this idea that some parts of you are desirable and others are not. All parts of you are desirable. Both "negative" and "positive" thoughts are essential to the human experience. Whatever we reject becomes even more powerful. If you embrace that all those "bad" thoughts that come up every now and then are just thoughts arising out of different parts of you, and you seek to understand the pain, frustration, and suffering this part is experiencing, those thoughts would cease to bother you.

Sometimes I feel extremely angry at my mother to the point that I want to hurt her emotionally and psychologically. Society tells us that we should never have such thoughts towards anyone, definitely not toward the person who has given birth to us. The problem with this kind of thinking is that it denies our humanness. If people were brutally honest, we'd know for sure that there isn't a single person on the planet who doesn't feel the urge to hurt another person at one point or another.

Most of the time, this desire or instinct to hurt another arises out of our own woundedness. In my case, I had an extremely difficult childhood. I didn't have the kind of childhood where my parents would be constantly doting on me. Instead, I felt lonely, unheard, and unacknowledged growing up. It seemed like I and my needs just didn't matter. As a child, I wasn't able to voice how I felt. Even if I tried to express myself, I was told to shut up. This created a lot of inner frustration and anger.

Once I started understanding that the part of me which wants to hurt my mother is really the wounded inner child whose needs weren't met, I can have more empathy for myself. I am also able to embrace the experience of having such thoughts and emotions arise in me as something "normal." It is perfectly normal to feel the way I do at times because of the kind of life experiences I had. Now, I am not making excuses for bad behavior or for actually hurting someone else. Having thoughts like that when you have been wounded and hurt is normal but as a human being, you have the choice to embrace the thoughts and emotions without acting on them.

Embracing your "negative" thoughts and emotions by trying to understand the parts of you that have been wounded and hurt can help you forge a deeper more meaningful relationship with yourself. The most important relationship in life is not with anyone else but with your own self. You must invest in this relationship because it is one relationship that is guaranteed to bring huge returns throughout your life. The relationship you have with yourself sets the ground for your relationships with other people. You can never have a better relationship with anyone else without first having an incredible relationship with yourself.

You have to be there for yourself. You must hear, acknowledge, and fully embrace who you are. All parts of you make you who you are. There isn't a single part of you that is undesirable, unwanted or bad. There are parts of you that are concerned for you that want to protect you. By acknowledging the thoughts and emotions which arise from them (which society labels as "negative" or "bad") you are embracing yourself fully. All parts of you are beautiful. It is our real and perceived imperfections that make us unique. The wide spectrum of emotions and thoughts we experience throughout a lifetime defines our humanness. For a truly fulfilling and rewarding life, we have to be completely at home with ourselves – with all parts of us.

Once I fully started embracing the "negative" thoughts and feelings I had towards my mother, I started understanding that part of me which was deeply wounded. As I healed this part of me by understanding its needs and trying to meet it as best as possible now as an adult, I was also able to have compassion for my mother. I understood that she was doing the best that she was capable of but her own dysfunctional childhood made her the type of person she was. I let go of my desire to seek some kind of redemption for the child-hood I never had.

I can't go back in time but I can use the challenging and painful experiences of my life to become better in the here and now. The greatest secret to a successful life is to master the art of turning your weaknesses into strengths, your pain, and challenges into blessings. My relationship with my mother isn't perfect and it is never going to be but I am at peace with my life – that's what matters!

EXERCISE

For the next three days, write down all the "negative" thoughts and feelings you are experiencing. You can create a dedicated journal for this practice and carry it with you everywhere. Whenever a negative thought or emotion comes up, write it down immediately. Seek to really hear yourself. Write down which part of you is trying to communicate with you and what they are trying to say.

For instance, that part of you which tells you not to get on a stage and give a speech may be trying to protect you from the pain and embarrassment you faced a long time ago when you spoke on stage as a child. Hear that part of you and say to yourself, "I hear you." Embrace the thought and feeling fully instead of trying to suppress it or run away from it. Very soon, it will go away on its own very much like how a wave arises and subsides of its own accord on the seabed.

5

YOUR EXTERNAL SUPPORT
SYSTEM

"Finally, be kind to yourself and have a good support system."

— NIKKI DELOACH

Having a reliable support system is absolutely essential for effectively managing our emotions and thoughts. There are two types of support systems: external and internal. Your external support system consists of friends, family, mentors, therapists, and others who are there for you when you need help. Your internal support comprises your ability to self-soothe.

290 | S. S. LEIGH

You can't always rely on others to give you what you want. Even if someone wanted to, it really isn't possible for any person in the world to be there for us a hundred percent of the time. Of course, we should express our needs to others in an authentic and honest way. That's how a great relationship is built. But we must also always have the ability to self-soothe.

In this chapter, we'll focus on external support systems for now. In the next chapter, I will teach you how you can build and strengthen your internal support system. Again, I want to emphasize that no thought or emotion is "bad." Whatever we suppress becomes even more potent at the subconscious level and continues to bother us in ways we may not consciously understand.

We have to be willing to accept, acknowledge, and face all the emotions that arise inside. No thought or feeling is bad – thoughts and feelings just are. They are there to help us experience life fully. Life can never be fully experienced without embracing the full spectrum of emotions and thoughts. Don't suppress or reject what comes up. Instead, seek to dive deep into yourself to learn more.

When you have the right kind of internal and external system, it becomes easy to manage all our thoughts and emotions without suppression. Without the right kind of internal and external support system, you may look for help at all the wrong places or you will seek to numb your-self. Hence, having a strong support system isn't a luxury but an absolute necessity for living a meaningful and fulfilling life.

GETTING TO THE ROOT OF THINGS

I cannot emphasize enough the fact that we are the sum total of our life experiences. How our primary caregivers responded to us in early life sets the stage for all our close personal relationships throughout life including the relationship we have with ourselves. If your childhood was fraught with trauma, you will have difficulty managing your emotions and thoughts. This is nothing to be ashamed of. It is a natural response to unmet needs and to the feeling of "not being seen."

Even if you had a fairly happy childhood where your needs were met and you felt seen, chances are there were certain parts of yourself you weren't able to express. Maybe you were chastised every time you expressed anger. From those experiences, you learned that anger is "bad" so now you deny the emotion of anger whenever it arises as a natural response to certain situations.

Again, no emotion is bad. Every emotion is there to help us fully experience life as a human being. Anger is a natural and very human response to situations we find unpleasant or where we feel threatened. Anger doesn't go away when it is suppressed. The only way to release it (and any difficult emotion for that matter) is by fully experiencing it. Keep in mind that acting out of anger and fully experiencing the feeling of anger are two completely different things altogether. I am not asking you to do the former. Acting in anger or out of anger is not healthy and can severely damage your personal relationships.

I am suggesting that you acknowledge your anger and look within to find out what it is trying to communicate to you. For instance, when I was little my mother would often shout at me for no fault of my own. She was frustrated with her own life and her marriage. Since I was a child, it was easy for her to take it out on me. I am not saying that she was doing it intentionally but there is no denying that these screaming episodes caused considerable damage to me and the experience of being shouted upon lived with me long through my adult life.

When my mother would scream at me for no reason, I would feel very angry. I also felt violated because I was unfairly being treated badly. As anger seethed in me, I tried confronting her a few times asking her what exactly had I done wrong. The truth was she didn't know why she was behaving the way she was. My questions would only exacerbate her frustration and anger. She would shout back saying, "How dare you ask me such a question! Shut up or I'll give you something to cry about."

From this experience, my inner child learned that anger was something "bad." I started suppressing all my negative feelings because I was afraid of upsetting my mother and

EMOTIONAL REGULATION SKILLS TO OVERCOME TOXIC T... | 293

making her anger even worse. I often walked on eggshells trying very hard not to upset her. No matter how hard I tried, she would find one reason or another to shout at me and scold me. I started suppressing my needs because asking her to meet any of them meant trouble.

From my childhood experiences, I learned that certain emotions and thoughts were "bad." I felt guilty whenever I felt angry or I wanted to say something nasty to my mother or anyone else whose behavior made me feel hurt. I also internalized the idea that my needs didn't matter. I became an over-giving excessively selfless person. The problem with being such a person is that it never comes from a place of authenticity. It is a classic trauma-based response.

Every person has needs and it is our right to expect others to meet them. Of course, we can't demand that others give us what we want – we can only politely ask for it. Some people won't give us what we want but there are more than 8 billion people on the planet. There certainly are many people in this world who are eager to give us what we want. We have to make ourselves good receivers by accepting graciously what is given to us and by also learning to politely ask for our needs to be met.

Irrespective of the kind of childhood you had, we all need to heal the inner child. Most people think of trauma only as something very extreme like being sexually or physically abused but trauma is a very individual experience. Trauma is any kind of mental, emotional, and spiritual scar that needs to be healed.

Maybe you had fantastically supportive parents but you had a few episodes in school where you were mocked by other students and that caused you to suppress certain parts of yourself. It is your job to find out which parts of your inner child you have suppressed or shut down. This is what lies at the root of all our problems with managing thoughts and emotions.

The thoughts and emotions we perceive as problems are simply parts of us that are seeking to be heard and validated. There is no shortcut to building thought and emotional regulation skills without healing the parts of us that have been suppressed and wounded in some way.

EXERCISE

Write down all those thoughts and emotions that you currently perceive as undesirable. If you need more space, feel free to use additional sheets of paper to note down everything. You want to be as thorough as possible.

_____

_____

_____

_____

Pick up one thought/emotion that bothers you the most and dive deep into how your problems with it started. I would recommend that you set aside around an hour to be completely by yourself. Create a relaxing atmosphere for yourself by practicing deep breathing (breathe deeply in on a count of 1-2-3-4 and breathe out gradually on a count of 1-2-3-4).

You can also play some relaxing music in the background and light some incense to help yourself relax. When you are ready close your eyes and go back to a time when you started internalizing the idea that the particular thought/emotion is bad. Try to recall the incident fully in as much detail as possible. When you are ready, open your eyes and write down everything you found out.

If no clear memory emerges, then simply observe whatever comes up. When someone has experienced severe trauma, they may not be able to recall anything at all as the mind may prevent them from recalling it so they don't have to relive the severe trauma. If this is happening with you, then just be patient with yourself. Observe whatever feelings, thoughts, and ideas come up and note those down.

Close your eyes and observe where in your body, you feel these thoughts/emotions. Unexpressed suppressed emotions get stored in the different parts of the body. They often manifest as aches and pains or other maladies. By scanning your body mentally with closed eyes, you'll be able to identify where exactly you feel these suppressed thoughts and emotions. When you are ready, open your eyes and note down your findings.

_____

_____

_____

_____

_____

_____

_____

_____

Now, go back to that incident from where the suppression began. In case you can't recall the actual incident, then just allow yourself to simply "be" with whatever is coming up. Become mindful of all the sensations that are happening in the body. Observe how the suppressed emotions have been stored in the body. If you are able to replay the incident in your mind, then relive it fully. Observe how you felt in that exact moment – where in your body you felt all the emotions and thoughts. As you are reliving the situation, instead of suppressing how you are feeling, embrace your thoughts and emotions fully.

298 | S. S. LEIGH

Say to yourself, "I acknowledge you. I accept you. All your thoughts and feelings are justified." Repeat this sentence to yourself as many times as needed. Be there for yourself. Whatever you needed at the time from others, you can now give to yourself. Give yourself the gift of understanding and acceptance.

This is a very powerful exercise. You can repeat it as many times as needed. I would recommend that you do it for all the thoughts and emotions you have suppressed. In order to gain mastery over your mind and your emotions, you have to first experience them fully without the seeking to suppress anything. By simply being fully present with them, you initiate the healing process.

YOUR EXTERNAL SUPPORT SYSTEM

We all need people around us who understand and support us. I am sure you have at least one person in your life right now or you had someone like that in the past. If you feel there is no one in your life who understands and supports you, then there is a lot of work to be done. Keep in mind, the people we surround ourselves with are always similar to us in some way.

If you don't have anyone in your life right now who wants to be there for you, then most likely you are surrounding your-self with people who are wounded and preoccupied with themselves. The solution lies in healing yourself. I'll suggest that you focus on building your internal support system for now. As you heal and evolve, in the external world, people will appear who will be aligned with who you would have become by then.

If you already have at least one person in your life who supports you and understands you, then I want to focus on how you can get the best out of that connection. When we are wounded and preoccupied with our own unmet needs, we don't communicate effectively. The other person may sincerely want to help us but people are not mind readers. We can't expect others to know our needs without us expressing them. I want to empower you with the skills you need to assert yourself and express your needs.

Your needs are important. You are important. You must learn to express what you want with clarity and honesty. That's how you will strengthen your external support system so others can help you in your journey the way you want to be helped. I am also going to share with you ideas for intentionally building and expanding your external support system.

EXPRESS YOUR NEEDS USING "I" STATEMENTS

What's the best way of making sure the other person won't do anything for you? Tell them how they never do anything for you – you'll pretty much be guaranteed that they won't do anything for you. Most of us are not taught how to communicate our needs effectively. We don't know how to express our difficult thoughts and emotions in a way that others would empathize with.

If you can relate, then don't despair. It isn't just you. Most people have no idea how to process and express whatever is bothering them. Chances are you were given the silent treatment or maybe your primary caregivers screamed at you every time you tried to express those thoughts and feelings. The good news is that effective clear communication is a skill that anyone can learn at any age.

You must also understand that we often overestimate how much time people spend thinking about us. The truth is we are all preoccupied with ourselves. One of the greatest life skills you can learn is the ability to not take things personally. Don't read too much into people's behavior and attribute meaning that isn't actually there.

If you want someone to do something for you, then you must ask for it clearly and honestly. Yes, there is always a 50% chance they won't do what you want but there is also a 50% chance that they may give you what you want. If you won't ask for what you want, then chances are almost null that you'll get exactly what you want.

So what exactly does it mean to be able to express your needs using "I" statements? Let us say you want to talk about how frustrated you are with work. You ask your spouse to listen to you – they start offering you solutions but that's not what you want. You just wanted them to validate your emotions and empathize with you. In the past, you would get frustrated and say things like, "You just don't understand me."

This statement sounds accusative. It would immediately make your spouse defensive – they were trying the best from their perspective. Even though they want to be there for you, they just don't know how. Feeling attacked isn't going to help redeem the situation much. Now, how about you employ a different approach and say to them, "Darling, I really want to vent about my tough day at work. I don't want to discuss solutions right now. I just want you to listen to me and empathize with me."

With this statement, you are telling them exactly what you want. There is no room for guesswork here. Most of the problems in relationships happen because people want the other person to read their mind. No one can do that. You have to maximize your chances of getting your needs met by clearly expressing exactly what it is you want from the other person. This is just one scenario but you can apply it to any situation.

These are the golden rules of effective communication:

- Use 'I" statements. "I would like you to..." "I would appreciate it if you..."
- Tell the other person exactly what they can do for you. Don't be demanding. Simply state what you want without pressurizing them to meet your needs.
- Explain how it will help you or how their doing what you want would add value to your life.
- When someone gives you what you want, be sure to express your gratitude. What gets rewarded, gets repeated!

BE WILLING TO HAVE DIFFICULT CONVERSATIONS

Most people shy away from difficult conversations. They suppress their emotions and needs until one day the lid blows off and they explode. Nothing good comes out of suppressing your own feelings and needs. You have to get comfortable being uncomfortable. Life is never fulfilling in the comfort zone. The more you step out of your comfort zone, the more you'll grow. The more you grow, the more fulfilling your life will be.

As I said earlier, when you state your needs, there is always a 50-50 chance it will be met but if you never state it, then chances are you'll never get what you want. I know how tough it can be to have these conversations, especially if you didn't grow up in a household where such communication was appreciated or engaged in. But now, as an adult, you are fully in charge of how you live your life. You deserve to have your needs met!

Very often I visualize initiating these difficult conversations as akin to jumping in a pool. I like to use Mel Robbins' five-second rule for taking action and beating procrastination (Robbins, 2017). So I just count 5-3-2-1 and do it. The more time you spend contemplating doing it, the more time your mind will have to talk you out of doing it. It is also painful to remain in such a state of limbo. You just need to give your-self an initial push like how you would do before jumping into the pool.

There is something incredibly freeing about being able to express your own truth even if the other person doesn't end up giving you what you want. The fact that you expressed what you wanted helps you feel liberated. Also, this kind of honest and open communication reveals to you who your true well-wishers are and who isn't truly there for you. The people who value you and love you will remain with you no matter what. They will try their best to meet your needs without sabotaging their own. But if you don't ask, the answer is always going to be "No."

EXERCISE

What is it that you want from others but you have never tried asking for it? Pick one thing that would make the greatest difference to your life right now and then commit to having that tough conversation. If that sounds too intimidating, then pick something where the stakes are pretty low. Ask for something that you don't care so much about but it would still be nice if you could have it.

As you gain practice and reap the benefits of your efforts, you'll want to repeat the process in other areas of your life where the stakes are higher and the outcome would make a tremendous difference to your life. If you find yourself procrastinating, visualize jumping into the swimming pool. Hold your breath, count till five and just do it!

After having the conversation, come back here and write down how you felt after having the conversation. I am sure you'll realize just how liberating it is to have such an open and honest conversation. Start turning this into a habit. Try to have an honest and open conversation with everyone who matters in your life.

SEEK OUT OTHERS WHO CAN HELP YOU

It is also a great idea to intentionally keep expanding your external support system by seeking those who have similar goals to you and others who can mentor you. How to do it practically? Thanks to the internet, it is easier than ever to meet people from all over the world with a few clicks of a button. You can find forums and support groups related to just about any topic. You can also meet people locally in clubs dedicated to a common interest. When you meet people with similar passions, interests, and struggles, chances are high they will understand you and you will be able to understand them.

It is also a good idea to work with or just be around coaches, mentors, therapists, and other experts from whom you can learn various skills. You can gain access to them by buying their books, attending courses, doing one-on-one sessions, etc. Yes, this will most likely require some kind of financial investment from your end but investing in yourself is one type of investment that always pays off great dividends. If you aren't sure, then start with books and free resources online like YouTube videos, podcasts, etc.

EXERCISE

In which area of your life do you need help right now? Look up online and offline groups, forums, etc. where you can meet others who have similar goals as you. Look up mentors, coaches, and experts in this area and start learning from them.

6

UNDERSTANDING NEEDS AND BOUNDARIES

"Boundaries define us. They define what is me and what is not me. A boundary shows me where I end and someone else begins, leading me to a sense of ownership. Knowing what I am to own and take responsibility for gives me freedom. Taking responsibility for my life opens up many different options. Boundaries help us keep the good in and the bad out."

— HENRY CLOUD

I decided to dedicate an entire chapter to boundary setting because this is an aspect of emotional regulation that often gets ignored. Emotional regulation is not about not having certain types of emotions or forcing yourself to feel certain emotions. Emotional regulation is about giving yourself a safe space to feel all your emotions irrespective of judgment and resistance.

Feeling your emotions by acknowledging, accepting, and even embracing them to a certain extent doesn't imply you have to act on them. This is where boundaries come into play. The boundaries you have with yourself and with others help you operate with awareness and self-control while you still maintain a safe space to feel the full spectrum of your emotional world.

As I always say, the key to emotional regulation is intense self-awareness. This same idea applies to boundary setting. You can set clear boundaries with others only when you know who you are, what you stand for, and what you want. Too many people are afraid to do this because they fear losing the relationship with the other person or upsetting others.

Trust me, no relationship is worth compromising with your boundaries for. You have the right to say "No." But you can say "no" with firmness and conviction only when you know what your own needs and priorities are. I'm not saying this is going to be easy. Once you start setting firm and clear boundaries, you'll certainly receive a lot of backlash from the people who benefitted from your lack of boundaries in the past.

You have to be prepared to be called "mean" and "selfish." Just know that being called "nice" is often not a compliment and certainly not something to be proud of. A lot of times it means you are allowing others to take from you whatever they want at the expense of your own needs and well-being. If you want to live a truly fulfilling life, you have to master the art of saying no. Your desire to care for yourself and your well-being must become stronger than your desire to be liked by others.

WHAT DOES IT MEAN TO HAVE STRONG BOUNDARIES?

I want to give you a definition that you can refer to which will help you assess how you are doing with establishing and maintaining personal boundaries. I would say a boundary is a real or perceived line around your property (including both your body/mind/soul and your material possessions in the external world) that should not be crossed under any circumstance.

We live in a society where having a fence around our physical property is the norm but no one teaches us how to have strong boundaries that protect our mind, body, and soul. In fact, there is a lot of guilt associated with boundary setting. A lot of people think that establishing boundaries makes them selfish. From a young age, this idea gets embedded in their psyche by teachers and parents who themselves lacked strong boundaries.

You are taught that to be "good," you must pander to other people's wishes even at the expense of your own mental, emotional, physical, and spiritual well-being. Hence, once you start setting boundaries as an adult, you encounter a lot of old programming that makes you think it is "bad" to have boundaries. Mastering the art of boundary setting requires a tremendous amount of unlearning. You have to let go of old ways of relating that are no longer serving you.

It is going to be very tough practicing emotional regulation skills if you are constantly allowing your desire to please others precedes over prioritizing your own needs and well-being. A lot of emotional issues people face in life is because they are constantly ignoring their own needs, desires, wants, and goals. Just because you are taught to live a certain way doesn't mean it is the right way to be or what's best for you.

Every time you do something and it just doesn't feel quite "right" in your gut, you know you are going against your nature and your needs. I am not talking about the kind of discomfort that comes from doing a difficult or challenging task – that may be painful but it leaves you feeling better about yourself. Every time you push your boundaries in order to grow and evolve into a higher version of yourself, the resultant satisfaction and self-esteem far outweigh the discomfort you experienced.

On the other hand, when you say yes to something that requires you to compromise your needs and your values, the experience leaves you feeling depleted and drained. If you keep denying your own needs and continue going against your core values, eventually, you'll build a huge reservoir of resentment and anger. It is only a matter of time before you'll blow up and experience rage toward the people you resent and are angry at.

Being a person with strong boundaries implies asserting your needs and pursuing your self-interest. I know that this is frowned upon by society. You are likely thinking, "Are you not asking me to be selfish by suggesting that I assert my needs and pursue my self-interests?" Valid question – I used to think the same way! It took me a long time to arrive at this understanding that looking after my own needs and protecting my personal boundaries doesn't make me selfish. Think of what happens when you say yes to someone else at the expense of your own self. You do what you think is right but internally, you start building resentment.

Also, most people don't say what they want because healthy communication is a skill that the majority never learn. Asserting your needs doesn't imply being mean and demanding. It means you tell others what they can do for you and then you give them the choice to give you what you need or not give it to you. Most people will never ask others what they want because they are too afraid of rejection. But think of it like this – if you never ask, chances are negligible that you'll ever receive what you want.

Even if you don't get what you want, at least you'll have the satisfaction of knowing you tried. Besides, you didn't have what you wanted in the first place so not having it after you have asked doesn't make you worse off. But what if you asked for something and you received it? Isn't it worth trying? After all, there is always at least a 50% chance that you may receive what you are asking for. If you don't ask, you'll likely never find out what you may have received by being vocal and upfront!

Asserting your needs comprises both asking for what you want from someone else and also for what you don't want them to do. A lot of times people have no idea that their actions, behavior, or words may be impacting us in the wrong way. Most people remain quiet and never express the truth about how they are feeling. This causes rifts in relationships while also having a negative impact on overall personal satisfaction.

On the other hand, telling others how they can make you more comfortable and at ease in their presence will help you build deeper connections with others. Being able to say you don't like something or don't want something is one of the most important boundary-setting skills that you must acquire if you want to live a fulfilling life.

EXERCISE

What are the needs that you are ignoring right now?

_____

_____

_____

_____

How often do you stay "yes" to things you don't want to do? Why do you think you do it?

_____

_____

_____

_____

What is preventing you from saying how you truly feel about the thing you are being asked to do? What are you afraid of? What do you fear will happen if you say "no"?

_____

_____

_____

_____

_____

Are you compromising with your core values to meet other people's needs and demands? What are these core values that you are compromising on right now?

_____

_____

_____

_____

_____

_____

How do you feel when you say "yes" to a demand or request you don't want to meet? Think of the last time you did it and try to recall everything you felt in your body. In which part of your body did you feel the maximum discomfort? Describe that feeling in as much detail as possible. Next time, you find yourself saying "yes" to something you'd much rather say "no" to observe what happens in your body and make note of it.

_____

_____

_____

_____

_____

Is it easy for you to tell others what you want from them? Write down the reasons that prevent you from asking others to give you what you would like to have.

_____

_____

_____

_____

_____

_____

Do you feel your needs and boundaries are important or do you feel you must keep "sacrificing" putting your own needs on the back burner in order to serve others?

_____

_____

_____

_____

_____

_____

Go back to your childhood and write down how your primary caregivers responded to you every time you said "no" to something you didn't want to do. How did it make you feel? What was the message that you received and internalized from their response to you?

Go back to your childhood and write down how your primary caregivers responded to you every time you asserted your boundaries by telling them what is acceptable to you and what is not. How did it make you feel? What was the message that you received and internalized from their response to you?

UNDERSTANDING YOUR RESPONSES TO THE EXERCISE ABOVE

I hope you have completed the exercises from the previous section. If not, I would urge you to go back and complete them. This section will help you dive deeper into your responses so you can understand why you are the way you are but reading it without an understanding of your own behavior and mindset patterns won't help you much.

As I always say, transformation happens through action. Reading and absorbing new information is important but it has real value only when we implement the wisdom we have extracted from the words we have read or heard.

The most fascinating thing about psychology is that it helps us understand why we are the way we are. The answer can often be traced back to early life. Our early childhood experiences lay down the foundation for how we show up in the world and interact with it as adults.

The stability of a child's early life has profound effects on physical and mental health, and unstable parent-child relationships, as well as abuse, can lead to behavioral disorders and increased mortality and morbidity from a wide variety of common diseases later in life (McEwen, 2003).

If you have trouble acknowledging and catering to your needs as an adult, you actually learned this behavior pattern long ago from your relationship with your primary caregivers. This isn't about blame but about understanding. When we understand how our behavior pattern was formed, we realize that most of the actions we engage in are learned responses.

If we can learn dysfunctional behavior patterns, then we can also unlearn them. I'm not saying it is easy but it is certainly worthwhile and most definitely possible. You can train yourself to think, act, respond, and behave like the person you have always wanted to be. You have the right to live life on your own terms and be whoever you wish to be.

Going back to the subject of early childhood experiences, if you grew up feeling like your needs don't matter, you would continue the same pattern into your adult connections. To change things, you must become conscious of what your needs and values are. Living a fulfilling life does require intense self-awareness. Expressing and asserting your needs effectively is a learnable skill but to get the most out of it, you must be aware of your values and goals. Who are you? Who you do you want to be? What are the goals you want to accomplish right now?

When you know the answer to the above questions (at least with some degree of clarity) asserting yourself in your relationships with others becomes simpler. A lot of times people don't express their needs because they fear rejection. Maybe you expressed your needs to your parents as a child and they responded with anger and violence.

Their response taught you that expressing your needs was dangerous and it should be avoided as much as possible. As an adult, if you express your needs most people won't respond in such an extreme way but the fear of such an intense reaction has become internalized in your system.

The solution lies in becoming self-aware. You have to get past stories of who you think you are and adopt new ways of being. In other words, you need to shift your mindset and start reprogramming yourself by building a skill set that you could not acquire from your early childhood environment. Trust me, there are many people in this world who would love to give you what you want.

You just need to identify who these people are and express your needs to them. Of course, there will be times when you won't receive what you ask for. When that happens, you must respect other people's boundaries and always remember that asking others for what you want doesn't obligate them to give it to you.

It simply gives them an opportunity to bestow upon you a gift that you truly want but as sovereign beings they have the right to refuse it. You don't have to force anyone to give you what you want. Don't get fixated on people – just know that for every person who says no to you, there is someone in the world who would eagerly say yes.

You just need to keep doing what's best for you – openly and honestly expressing your needs. Even if you get rejected, you won't die of it. As a child, conforming to your environment by suppressing your own needs was essential to your survival but you are no longer that child. You are an adult who has the power to remove themselves from any environment that isn't suitable for them. You also have the power to recreate your environment and your social circle.

Besides, every time you do get your needs met, you are reinforcing a new pattern – a new way of being. With every positive experience, you are reprogramming yourself in a positive way. This brings you closer to your goals and to the person you want to be. Also, there is something incredibly liberating about expressing your own truth. When you speak out, you feel free even if the idea of speaking out was frightening initially. You also have the conviction and the satisfaction that you tried your best irrespective of the result that you get. However, once you start doing this, you'll be surprised by how frequently people are actually eager to give you what you want, especially those who truly love you and care for you.

STOP OVER-GIVING

We live in a world where we are constantly bombarded by this idea of giving, giving, giving... Most people have become really good at giving but there is an essential life skill they never learned – how to receive! So let me ask you this – how comfortable are you with receiving? Do you receive heartfelt gifts (whether material items, time, energy, compliments, etc.) gracefully or with guilt? Do you feel you deserve what you receive or you feel unworthy of them?

Most people don't get in life what they want because deep inside they feel unworthy of it. If that sounds like you, then I want to say to you, "It is okay to feel this way!" We must acknowledge and embrace all our feelings, emotions, and thoughts. They are telling us where we have been, what we have learned, how we operate in the world according to the programming we have received. At the same time, we don't have to act on these feelings, thoughts, and emotions. We can retrain ourselves to show up differently in the world and in our relationships – including in our relationship with ourselves.

You are not good at receiving because no one taught you how to receive gracefully. If you are always the person who is giving, then you are not honoring the natural ebb and flow of life. Harmony and balance are the core principles upon with nature herself operates. When we refuse to receive with grace and gratitude, we are actually causing an imbalance in the natural flow of life. This is why we end up feeling so uneasy when we receive a beautiful gift someone wanted to give us. The other person also feels deprived and uneasy because they were stripped off an opportunity for doing something good for another human being.

322 | S. S. LEIGH

EXERCISE

How do you feel when someone wants to give you something?

_____

_____

_____

_____

_____

_____

How do you respond when someone compliments you?

_____

_____

_____

_____

_____

_____

Do you ask for help when you need it?

_____

_____

How do you feel when you receive something you ask for?
Do you feel worthy of it or do you feel guilty?

Do you apologize excessively every time you ask for help
and when you feel someone may be inconveniencing themselves to give you what you need?

HOW TO BE A GOOD RECEIVER

Like most things in life, being a good receiver is a skill that you develop through consistent practice. It doesn't matter how bad you have been at it so far, if you want to change, then nothing can prevent you from becoming an excellent receiver. Yes, we are talking about balance here. You want to be good at both giving and receiving. You must do good to others but you must also allow others to do good unto you.

So here's how you do it:

When someone offers you a compliment, don't sabotage it by explaining how their words are not true. It is akin to rejecting a beautifully wrapped present by throwing it back in the giver's face. Neither the giver nor the receiver feels enriched by such an experience. Instead, just say "thank you" with a smile. You also don't need to compliment them back. A compliment that is given to the other person as a response to their original compliment doesn't come across as genuine. Instead, just enjoy their gift. If you want to give them a genuine compliment, then reserve it for later. In this moment, just allow yourself to bask in the glory of the wonderful gift they have given you.

Use "I" statement to ask others for help. "I need…" "I want…" "I would appreciate it if you would…" "I would love it if you would…" Get rid of this idea that you are inconveniencing them by asking them for help. If they can't give you what you need, let them be the one to decide this. By asserting your needs, you are giving them a chance to do something for you. Trust that you are worthy of it and that doing something for you is not an obligation but something beautiful, pleasurable, and joyous for another human being.

Don't apologize excessively when someone does something for you. You are worthy of their time and energy. Start believing that they are just as enriched by the experience of giving you something you need as you have been enriched by it. A heartfelt "thank you" and a genuine appreciation for their efforts is all you need to give them in return.

EXERCISE

Ask someone to do something for you. Be polite, clear, and assertive. For example, if you feel overwhelmed preparing and serving dinner, then today ask your partner if they would help you in the process. Use I statements like, "Honey, I would really love it if you would help me chop the vegetables for dinner." "I would appreciate it if you would help me set the table."

Whatever it is you want, just ask for it clearly and when you receive it, trust that you absolutely deserve what you are receiving. If by any chance, you are met with a refusal, don't take it personally. When someone refuses you something it simply means they are unable to give you what you want right now. It doesn't diminish your value as a human being. However, most of the time, people will be happy to give you what you want provided you state your needs clearly and with "I" statements.

If you are really afraid of refusal, start by asking for small favors and when people give you what you want. Build up your muscle from there and then move on to the things that would really make a huge difference to your life.

7

HANDLING INTENSE EMOTIONS AND EMOTIONAL BREAKDOWNS

"Your emotions make you human. Even the unpleasant ones have a purpose. Don't lock them away. If you ignore them, they just get louder and angrier."

— SABAA TAHIR

In this chapter, I want to give you practical tools for handling emotions. I want you to have a toolkit with you for times of intense emotional turmoil. They are indeed part of the human experience. Building emotional regulation skills doesn't imply you will never experience intense emotions again. It is all about how you handle these intense emotions and your emotional world in general.

I have said this before and I will say it again. All your emotions are important. There is no such thing as an undesirable emotion. As human beings, we must allow ourselves to experience the full spectrum of emotions. It takes a great deal of maturity to sit with uncomfortable emotions, simply feeling and witnessing them. The harder you try to reject something, the stronger it will come back at you. The emotions you reject never go away. They simply slip deep inside your subconscious mind from where they continue to impact your mind, emotions, and behavior.

WHAT ARE INTENSE EMOTIONS?

That being said, there is a difference between experiencing intense emotions and having emotional breakdowns. Experiencing intense emotions implies undergoing a state of feeling powerful emotions. This includes both positive and negative emotions. You can feel just as overwhelmed with love and joy as you can be with anger and hate. Intense emotions can be overpowering and overwhelming in the sense that they can negatively impact your ability to function in daily life.

Intense emotions often trigger a fight-or-flight response leaving us with trepidation, sweating, and a palpitating heart. We all experience intense emotions every now and then. They can happen as a response to specific events, situations, people, and places. They can also result from a build-up of stress over time. In some cases, when a person perpetually and constantly experiences intense emotions to the extent that it becomes debilitating and dysfunctional, there can be other major issues lurking under the surface.

For instance, when a person perpetually and regularly responds to situations and events with emotions that are not in proportion to the event and situation itself, it can be a sign of depression, bipolar disorder, ADHD and other mental health conditions. There are also genetic factors that can make certain individuals more prone to intense emotions than others (Bergland, 2015). Hence, we can't always say that someone who perpetually experiences intense emotions has some kind of mental health condition. It can also just be a genetic predisposition that makes them a very emotionally intense person.

WHAT IS AN EMOTIONAL BREAKDOWN?

An emotional breakdown is a period of extreme emotional distress that causes severe disruption to a person's daily life. Emotional breakdowns can occur in the aftermath of a traumatic event or as a result of mental and emotional suppression over an extended period of time.

When a person is having an emotional breakdown they may lose their appetite, have debilitating anxiety, suffer from insomnia, and struggle to concentrate on even the simplest tasks of daily life. These are only some of the key character-istics of an emotional breakdown and not all of them.

During an emotional breakdown, people often feel like their life is spiraling out of control. They also find it really hard to control themselves. This can lead to abrupt spells of crying, shouting, screaming, angry outbursts, etc. They struggle to contain and manage their emotions. Everything feels out of control and it becomes hard and sometimes impossible to operate in daily life.

When a person is having an emotional breakdown, they may withdraw from all social interactions. They may also struggle with basic self-care like taking a shower, fixing a meal for themselves, etc. It is very important to have compassion for oneself when one is undergoing an emotional breakdown. It is also advisable to seek profes-sional help, especially if the breakdown continues for extended periods of time.

THE DIFFERENCE BETWEEN EXPERIENCING INTENSE EMOTIONS AND HAVING AN EMOTIONAL BREAKDOWN

The key difference between experiencing intense emotions and having an emotional breakdown lies in the duration of the experience and its impact on the individual. Intense emotions may be distressing and can somewhat disrupt a person's daily life but the individual still experiences a sense of relative control over their emotions and their life.

On the other hand, when someone is having an emotional breakdown, they may find it impossible to perform even the most basic tasks of daily life. This happens when a person's coping mechanisms become severely overwhelmed. It feels like life is completely spiraling out of control and the individual seems unable to control their own self.

It is important to note that learning to deal with intense emotions properly can help prevent the possibility of a complete breakdown. Events like the death of a loved one or severe loss of any kind are part of the human experience. Someone who hasn't developed the tools and trained their coping mechanisms to handle intense emotions can break down when an extreme event happens.

In this chapter, I want to empower you with the right kind of tools and techniques to manage intense emotions. By paying attention to your emotional world, you'll be able to live a more fulfilling life. Always remember that what doesn't get dealt with, gets stored somewhere else. Just because something is out of sight doesn't mean that it no longer impacts you. It is akin to stuffing all your clutter in one armoire. Your house may look clean on the surface but it is only a matter of time that the armoire will burst open and all the clutter will splatter all over your house once again.

332 | S. S. LEIGH

I will also give you the tools and techniques for managing an emotional breakdown. You'll know what to do if you or someone else is having an emotional breakdown. As I said earlier, if you get in the habit of regularly dealing with your intense emotions as they arise, you'll minimize the possibility of having an emotional breakdown.

THE CALL-IT-OUT ALOUD TECHNIQUE

I call this technique call it out aloud because that's exactly what you do. When you are experiencing distressing emotions, don't try to suppress them or deny them. Instead, focus on accepting and acknowledging them. Accepting distressing emotions doesn't mean you have to act on them or mull on them. It simply means accepting that you are experiencing certain emotions at the moment and IT IS OKAY to allow yourself to have this experience.

You start talking to yourself saying exactly what is happening. Ideally, you want to be able to speak out aloud to yourself but if that's not possible, then you can also do the talking silently inside your mind. I would still strongly recommend that you find a space where you can be by yourself and then just speak out aloud to yourself. This really helps with the disassociation practice. When you are speaking inside your mind, it is easier to become lost in the maze of thoughts.

So what does this look in practice? Let us say you are experiencing anger. You will say to yourself, "I feel anger – extreme anger right now." Allow yourself to feel the anger in its full intensity. Again, it isn't something to be discarded, denied or suppressed. Sit with it – let it communicate with you.

Continue identifying, labeling, and acknowledging whatever is happening. For instance, your narration can be something like, "I feel very upset right now. My palms are sweating, my breathing is erratic, my heart is palpitating. I am feeling a fight-or-flight reaction in its full intensity. I honestly feel a massive urge to punch my boss. I feel the urge to shout, "How dare you talk to me like that?"

You acknowledge all the negative and "bad" things you are feeling the urge to do. This doesn't mean you have to act on them. You are simply acknowledging and accepting that a part of you has been so severely affected by the situation that you are feeling the urge to do something drastic. Something really magical begins to happen when you start accepting all your feelings, emotions, and urges as they are. After a while, you lose the urge to act on those destructive thoughts that arise in a moment of heightened emotions.

Intense emotions fog our ability to think clearly. We may feel tempted to do something that we will likely regret later. It is crucial to put off taking important decisions until you are feeling more balanced. In fact, never take any important decision when you are in a heightened emotional state – be it positive or negative emotions. Both extreme joy and extreme dejection can obfuscate your ability to think clearly. Important decisions should only be taken in a state of emotional equilibrium when you are neither too over-whelmed by positive emotions nor too dragged down by negative emotions.

VENTING THROUGH WRITING

Writing is a very powerful medium for processing and venting difficult emotions. I am often amazed by how relieved I feel every time I write down what I am feeling. In a heightened emotional state, I feel the urge to do something that I know I will regret later but once I write down every-thing I am feeling, the urge also passes away. Many times I have written down my feelings, emotions, and thoughts and by the end I felt like a different person.

The process is very simple. You just take a pen and a paper and start writing everything that is on your thinking and feeling. Don't censor yourself – don't try to be perfect with your writing. The writing is only for you. You don't have to worry about grammar or spelling. Just express yourself on paper. Yes, I would recommend that you do this exercise on paper. According to a study conducted by University of Tokyo, it was found that writing on paper engages the brain more powerfully than what can be achieved by writing on digital devices (University of Tokyo, 2021).

Writing with digital tools just doesn't feel the same. It can help process your thoughts but I always feel a more powerful sense of release and relief when I pour my difficult thoughts and emotions on paper. I would also recommend ritually letting them go by burning or tearing the paper and releasing the ashes or pieces in a flowing water body. If you don't have access to a flowing water body, then you can simply flush the paper. Just be careful if you are flushing pieces of paper instead of just the ashes. It might clog your toilet. Alternatively, you can bury the ashes or pieces in earth. Do whatever helps you feel better!

DEEP BREATHING

When you are in a heightened emotional state, your breathing automatically becomes erratic. The body and mind are strongly connected. Hence, one of the ways to get yourself to calm down is by focusing on the body. By breathing deeply, you'll start feeling more centered and grounded.

When you are overwhelmed, just shift your focus from what is troubling you onto your breathing. I know it is going to be tough to let go of it but tell yourself it is just for a few moments. You can go back to it after a while. This will trick the mind into loosening the grip on to distressing thoughts and emotions. Also, keep in mind that by constantly focusing on your troublesome thoughts and emotions, you can't solve a challenging situation. Solutions require feeling centered and calm.

For a few moments, just sit down with yourself. Close your eyes and breathe deeply. You can count from 1-8 for each inhalation and exhalation. So inhale 1-2-3-4-5-6-7-8. Exhale 1-2-3-4-5-6-7-8. To engage your body and mind further, you can also do the counting with your fingers while focusing on your breath.

If you can't close your eyes, then do the exercise with your eyes open but do it, please! Although I would strongly recommend doing it with your eyes closed. It really helps disconnect from the chaos you may be experiencing in your external reality.

You can also do this breathing technique when you are about to burst out or lash out on someone. When you are feeling the urge to act on that instinct, buy yourself a few moments. Just practice this breathing technique by focusing entirely on your breathing. You aren't saying you won't do what you are feeling the urge to do. You are just buying yourself a few moments after which you will be free to do whatever you must do.

After doing the breathing exercises you will be amazed to realize that the urge to take drastic action would have passed away. If it doesn't, just buy yourself a few more moments and continue doing this exercise. Also, do the other practices I am sharing in this chapter. Eventually, the urge to take drastic action will surely pass away and you will be glad it did!

MOVE YOUR BODY

As I said earlier, the body and mind are strongly connected. Just as the body can be influenced with the mind, the mind can also be influenced by the body. Intense emotions often cause muscle stiffness and a sense of stagnancy in the body and mind. One powerful solution for overcoming this state is by simply moving the body. I would highly recommend taking walks in nature. The refreshing and replenishing air in nature really helps with feeling centered and grounded – doesn't matter whether you are taking a walk in a public park or a seashore.

That being said, any kind of proper movement is good for the body. The human body isn't designed to be confined to a desk and chair for extended periods of time. The body thrives on movement. It is also a well-known fact that exercise produces endorphins or feel-good hormones. Physical movement is directly linked with a significant reduction in stress (Mayo Clinic Staff, 2022).

Whatever your choice of movement is, just get your body moving. Don't sit around and continue dwelling on what's vexing you. Do some yoga, tai chi, stretching, gym workouts, or simply take a walk.

POSITIVE SELF-TALK

We are all constantly conversing with ourselves in the silent alleys of our minds. Unfortunately, in most cases, this self-talk is extremely negative. It tends to be a never-ending barrage of criticism and constantly disparaging yourself. You may think it is your own inner voice saying all this to you. Hence, you accept it as the truth.

Your inner critic isn't really you. It is an internalized voice of your primary caregiver. When you were a small child, you were constantly told who you are, what you are capable of, what you aren't capable of. You didn't have enough experience or perspective on life to form your own opinions. You simply accepted what was told to you. Of course, some of it will be good that supports you in living a healthy and fulfilling life. Unfortunately, in most cases, the inner critic is all too loud. It constantly tells you what you cannot do or criticizes you so harshly that you feel debilitated by it.

I am not suggesting that you should blame your primary caregivers. In most cases, parents want the best for their children. However, people are not perfect. Human beings have a tendency of projecting on to others what they believe to be true for themselves. If they believe they can't do something, they'll tell you that you can't do it either. We also can't ignore the fact that we live in a highly chaotic world. Very few people are truly in touch with themselves or have their intellectual and emotional lives together. Parents unwittingly pass on their unhealed trauma and dysfunctional behavior patterns onto their children.

The good news is that most of the negative behavioral and thought patterns we suffer from are things we have learned from others. If we can learn something negative unwittingly, then we can also unlearn it. With intention, purpose, knowledge, and determination, we can retrain ourselves to be the type of person we truly want to be. You have the power to live life on your own terms and be the highest version of yourself!

The first step you must take is to become aware of your self-talk. Throughout the day, pause for a few minutes every couple of hours, and ask yourself, "What am I thinking and feeling right now?" Observe what your mind is telling you. You can also use the narration technique I shared with you earlier to state to yourself what is going on with you.

Once you start spotting the negative self-talk, ask yourself, "Is this really true? What evidence do I have that this is true? What evidence I have that this is not true?" Once you start compelling yourself to think logically, you'll realize that most of the self-criticism is largely illogical. There is no basis for why you should believe those negative things about yourself.

However, the inner critic has been programmed over years. It isn't going to be defeated that easily. You must replace criticisms with positive self-talk. Let us assume this is what your inner critic is saying, "I am so bad at this. I just can't do anything right." You can replace this with, "I have the power and the ability to be good at anything I truly commit to. I know I can do anything I set my mind upon!" Say it out aloud to reinforce the idea further. If that's not possible, then simply keep repeating the new positive affirmation inside your mind.

You want to talk to yourself like your best friend. What will you say to your best friend if they were struggling with self-doubt or were constantly criticizing themselves? You also want to become your own greatest cheerleader. If you start feeling exhausted or self-doubt begins creeping in, encourage yourself like a cheerleader, "Come on, you can do this!" "You've got this. Keep going!" "I know I can do this!"

This kind of positive cheerleading will provide you the energy to keep pushing and preserving to achieve your goals.

HOW TO DEAL WITH AN EMOTIONAL BREAKDOWN

Having an emotional breakdown in the face of an extreme event is not something out of the ordinary. It is possible to overcome such a breakdown on your own, especially with the help of loving family members and friends. But if the breakdown persists for an extremely long duration to the extent that it cripples one's work and social life, it may become necessary to seek professional help.

In this section, I will highlight what you can do if you or someone you know is having an emotional breakdown. All the techniques I shared in the previous section are also useful for dealing with an emotional breakdown but here are some additional things that one should focus on when undergoing such a difficult experience.

FOCUS ON MAINTAINING A ROUTINE

I know how hard this is but you must make the effort to create a routine for yourself. Your daily routine is the first thing that goes out of the window when a breakdown occurs but one of the most effective techniques for bringing a sense of balance to your life is also by going back to that routine. Of course, it is going to be extremely challenging but simply doing what you need to do helps you move your body and that's what initiates the healing process.

Try to go to bed at a set time and wake up at a set time. I know this is easier said than done but you must make the effort. If you don't know how you are going to get through life, shift your focus to something smaller by asking yourself, "What's the one thing I need to do right now" and just do it. It can be something as simple as washing your plate and putting it back where it belongs or folding your clothes and putting them away.

Don't see your daily routine as a burden but as a means for finding comfort. You will find a sense of familiarity and a degree of harmony in maintaining your daily routine.

INVEST IN SELF-CARE

Be extremely gentle and compassionate with yourself – you deserve it. Take the time to look after yourself. Pamper yourself as much as you can. Cook your favorite meals if you can or allow yourself to order your favorite food. Never feel guilty about looking after yourself. You are worth the effort, time, money, and resources!

SPEND TIME WITH TRUSTED LOVED ONES

Try to spend time with others who love and support you. When you are with them don't just talk about all your distressing emotions and thoughts. Instead, focus on doing something fun together. For instance, you can go to an amusement park together or do something else that both parties enjoy. Spending time with loved ones is extremely therapeutic and healing.

JOIN SUPPORT GROUPS

More often than not, the only people who can truly understand what we are going through are other people who are either still undergoing a similar experience or who have been through it in the past. Finding a local or online support group for your specific issue can be an excellent resource for overcoming an emotional breakdown.

You can ask for assistance from people who have overcome similar challenges – learn what they did and try their methods and techniques for yourself. Try to learn as much as possible about how other people are coping with their challenges – what works for them and what doesn't. Support groups can really be an exceptional resource for finding practical solutions and techniques for overcoming one's challenges. You also find understanding and compassion with others who have been through or are going through something similar. That can truly be a huge blessing!

8

PRACTICING MINDFULNESS, MEDITATION, AND GUIDED JOURNALING EXERCISES

"The issues we often run away from and refuse to address, are the very things that end up transforming our lives when we choose and commit to healing from buried emotional wounds."

— KEMI SOGUNLE

In this chapter, I want to share with you some more practical tools that you can use in your daily life to overcome toxic thinking and dysfunctional behavior patterns. You can use these tools whenever you are feeling stressed and/or overwhelmed. You can also use them every day as daily practices to support yourself in living a healthy life.

The more often you do these practices, the greater will be the benefits you derive from them. But even if you do them only once in a while, they will help you calm down and regain focus.

The important thing to always remember is that difficult and painful emotions should never be suppressed. They should be faced, embraced, and dealt with. I have said this before and I will say it again. All your emotions are there to support you in living a full and meaningful life. Never fall for the temptation of shutting some away and embracing only a few. What gets suppressed continues to impact our life in ways we do not even recognize.

Most people live a life of incessant distraction. Thanks to the abundance of technology, it is easier now than ever to find a new distraction to constantly keep oneself preoccupied. I observe how people turn off the computer only to switch on the TV. When they finally turn off the TV, they pick up their phones whiling away endless hours meaninglessly browsing the internet. The internet is a wonderful place to learn new skills, acquire new knowledge, and connect with other interesting people. But undisciplined use of the internet can also be very damaging. The key word here is to be intentional with your time.

Whatever you are doing, do it with mindfulness. Don't watch TV or play video games only to distract yourself. In fact, distraction at its core is an instinct to avoid pain. For instance, you sit down to write a business report. The task is painful and requires you to concentrate. To avoid the pain, you seek distractions like checking your email or browsing social media.

I am not suggesting that you should give up TV, social media, or anything else. I am just advocating for using the tools available at your disposal with intention and purpose to create the kind of life YOU want to live. There is a difference between using these tools for your own benefit and allowing them to dominate your life because you didn't clarify how you should be utilizing them in the first place.

The same can be said for food. Don't eat when you are bored, tired, or in emotional pain. Eat to nourish your body. Feed yourself high-quality nutritious food that will support you in living a healthy life. Emotional eating is a huge problem in modern-day society. Most people eat way more than what their body actually needs and worse than that, they are eating food devoid of any real nutrition.

Research suggests that a wholesome Mediterranean diet can really help with emotional regulation (Holt, Lee, Morton, Tonstad, 2014). The Mediterranean diet focuses heavily on the consumption of whole grains, fruits, vegetables, nuts, beans, fish, and some meat. I would encourage you to focus on eating fresh wholesome food. Stay away from packaged meals that contain a lot of chemicals and additives. Living a healthy life requires thinking healthily.

Once you start focusing on making healthier choices, you will eat differently and make different choices. Try to move your body as much as possible. Instead of taking the elevator, take the stairs. Instead of munching on fries, opt for the apple. Initially, it may be difficult to make these healthy choices but over time, you will train your taste buds to start liking wholesome food items more.

PRACTICING MINDFULNESS

Most of our pain and suffering is often not in the present but in the memory of the past or in anticipation of the future. Mindfulness is a powerful practice because it allows you to fully inhabit the present moment. Instead of allowing your mind to wander here and there, you bring it to be fully present with your body in the here and now.

Most of our problems and suffering disappear when our consciousness fully inhabits the present moment. I really believe that heaven and hell reside within the mind. Untamed thoughts and emotions can give you the experience of living in hell. On the other hand, a calm and stable mind can give you the experience of heaven on earth.

Research also shows that mindfulness practices are extremely beneficial for managing emotional dysregulation (Guendelman, Medeiros, Rampes, 2017). In this section, I want to share with you a simple mindfulness practice that you can do any time of the day. You don't need to be in a specific type of place to do it nor do you need special props and tools. Mindfulness is the act of becoming fully present in the moment with whatever you are doing. It also increases your focus. Hence, it boosts your performance as well.

You can do this mindfulness exercise lying down or while sitting in a chair. You can also do it while taking a walk in nature or while doing gentle stretches. You can close your eyes if you are lying down or sitting in a chair. If you are taking a walk, then obviously you'll have to keep your eyes open. There are no rules except to just become present with yourself and inhabit the present moment fully.

THE PRACTICE

Find a place where you can be by yourself for this practice. Sit up straight if you are sitting up in a chair. If you are lying down or walking, then make sure that your back is straight. Before beginning the practice, it is important to get your body in proper posture. If possible, close your eyes.

Focus on your breath – notice how each breath is going in and observe how each breath comes out. Focus all your attention on the in-flow and out-flow of breath. Focus on your breathing as if the entire world has dissolved for now. All that exists in this moment is your breath – the in-flow and out-flow of breath is all there is for now.

With each inhalation, observe how the breath is entering through your nose gently touching your nostrils and then spreading through your entire body. As the breath spreads through your body, it is rejuvenating and replenishing each body part. Your body, mind, and soul are being transformed by the power of this breath. You are becoming the highest and finest version of yourself through the power of each inhalation.

As you exhale, feel all the accumulated tension, stress, pain, and suffering melting away. With each exhalation, release all that is unwanted. As the breath moves out of your body and exits through your nose, it is taking away with you everything that no longer serves you. You are feeling light, restful, and joyful as you have been freed from everything that was previously weighing you down.

Continue taking deep breaths, visualizing how each breath is filling you with hope, positivity, joy, and happiness. With each exhalation, continue releasing everything that no longer serves you. You can also visualize each in-breath as a fresh green-colored energy that enters your body to replenish and rejuvenate your body, mind, and soul. You can visualize each out breath as a dark brown-colored energy that you are expelling out of your system.

Continue breathing deeply – with each inhalation your chest and stomach expand. With each exhalation, your chest and stomach are contracting. Focus on this deep breathing. Your body and mind are becoming relaxed. If thoughts arise, witness them. Don't dismiss any thought. Don't cling on to any thought. Your mind is like an infinite ocean. Each thought is like a wave that arises and subsides of its own accord. You are sitting on the seashore simply watching the waves arise and subside.

Continue focusing on your breath but now also become aware of your surroundings. What are the sounds you can hear now? What are you smelling? What kind of taste do you have in your mouth right now? If your eyes are open, then observe what your eyes are seeing. Become fully present in the here and now. Observe the world around you without judging it. Just be present with it. Observe the world as if it were a movie playing out in front of your eyes. Just watch, feel, and experience it. Do not resist or reject anything.

For as long as you feel comfortable, you can continue doing this exercise. Remain focused on your breath and just observe both your inner and outer world. If any judgment or thought arises, witness it like a wave arising and subsiding in the vast ocean of your consciousness.

When you are ready, take a few more deep breaths to ground yourself. Rub your palms together, place them on your closed eyelids and gently open your eyes. If your eyes were open, then just move your body slightly vigorously.

MINDFULNESS ON THE GO

Practicing mindfulness as you go about your day is very powerful for remaining focused and doing your best at every task you undertake. Practicing mindfulness on the go is deceptively simple. I am saying "deceptively simple" because it seems very simple on the surface but that doesn't mean it is easy to practice. It does require a considerable amount of effort at least at the beginning. However, I would say it is totally worth the effort.

So what does mindfulness on the go look like? You can practice it anytime and anywhere. Just ask yourself "What am I doing right now?" "Where is my mind right now?" "Is my mind fully present with my body right now?" If you find your mind wandering, then gently bring it into the present moment to fully inhabit your body. Allow yourself to feel your body. For instance, if you are typing on your keyboard, then feel the sensation of your finger touching the keyboard fully.

If you are walking, allow yourself to feel what the ground beneath your feet feels like while you are walking. Being fully present inside your body means experiencing the present moment with all your five senses. The easiest way to get yourself to fully inhabit your body and the present moment is by focusing on what your five senses are communicating to you. What are you seeing? What are you smelling? What are you hearing? What are you tasting? What are you touching?

You can practice this while doing any task. It will compel you to be fully present with and focus on whatever you are doing. This is the key to productivity!

STRESS RELEASE MEDITATION

Mental and emotional stress can make you very dysregulated. To practice emotional regulation, it is very important that you release stress from the body and mind on a regular basis. You can record this meditation in your own voice and listen to it every day or whenever you are feeling particularly stressed out.

I would highly recommend that you maintain a dedicated corner in your house for practicing meditation. This way, in your mind, that space will become associated with stress release and relaxation. Every time you sit down or lie down there, your mind will signal to your body it is time to relax. Yes, you can do this exercise in bed as well but I would recommend having a separate corner in your house set aside for meditation. The goal is also to remain in a state of relaxed wakefulness throughout the meditation and not to fall asleep. Since your bed is associated with sleeping, it is highly likely that you will fall asleep while doing the meditation practice.

That being said, if you have trouble sleeping, then you can certainly use this meditation as a tool to manage your insomnia. In that case, you can definitely do it in bed lying down. I would still recommend that you additionally practice it solely as a meditation practice for deep relaxation at another time of the day as well. This will help you train your body to remain in a state of relaxed wakefulness throughout the day and over time, you'll build the skill to evoke such a state at will.

THE PRACTICE

Find a quiet space where no one will disturb you. Sit down comfortably and close your eyes.

Focus your mind on your breathing. Breathe deeply. With each inhalation, your chest and stomach expand. With each exhalation, your chest and stomach contract. To keep your mind focused you can count to 8 for each inhalation and exhalation. Inhale 1-2-3-4-5-6-7-8. Exhale 1-2-3-4-5-6-7-8. Continue breathing deeply. With each inhalation, feel yourself getting renewed and refreshed. With each exhalation, release all the tension and accumulated stress from your body and mind.

Now that you are feeling grounded and centered, take your focus to your toes. Feel your toes. If there is tension, release it with the next exhalation. As you inhale, say to yourself, "I am relaxing my toes. My toes are completely relaxed." As you exhale, release all stress and tension from your toes.

Focus on the soles of your feet and release any tension you are feeling right now. As you inhale, say to yourself, "I am relaxing the soles of my feet. The soles of my feet are completely relaxed." As you exhale, release all stress and tension from the soles of your feet.

Focus on the top of your feet and release any tension you are feeling right now. As you inhale, say to yourself, "I am relaxing the top of my feet. The top of my feet are completely relaxed." As you exhale, release all stress and tension from the top of your feet.

Focus on your ankles and bottom legs. As you inhale, say to yourself, "I am relaxing my ankles and bottom legs. My ankles and bottom legs are completely relaxed." As you exhale, release all stress and tension from your ankles and bottom legs.

Focus on your upper legs. As you inhale, say to yourself, "I am relaxing my upper legs. My upper legs are completely relaxed." As you exhale, release all stress and tension from your upper legs.

Focus on your hips. As you inhale, say to yourself, "I am relaxing my hips. My hips are completely relaxed." As you exhale, release all stress and tension from your hips.

Focus on your stomach and lower back. As you inhale, say to yourself, "I am relaxing my stomach and lower back. My stomach and lower back are completely relaxed." As you exhale, release all stress and tension from your stomach and lower back.

Focus on your chest and upper back. As you inhale, say to yourself, "I am relaxing my chest and upper back. My chest and upper back are completely relaxed." As you exhale, release all stress and tension from your chest and upper back.

Focus on your wrist and palms. As you inhale, say to yourself, "I am relaxing my wrist and palms. My wrist and palms are completely relaxed." As you exhale, release all stress and tension from your wrist and palms.

Focus on your elbows and lower arms. As you inhale, say to yourself, "I am relaxing my elbows and lower arms. My elbows and lower arms are completely relaxed." As you exhale, release all stress and tension from your elbows and lower arms.

Focus on your upper arms. As you inhale, say to yourself, "I am relaxing my upper arms. My upper arms are completely relaxed." As you exhale, release all stress and tension from your upper arms.

Focus on your shoulders and neck. As you inhale, say to yourself, "I am relaxing my shoulders and neck. My shoulders and neck are completely relaxed." As you exhale, release all stress and tension from your shoulders and neck.

Focus on your eyes and face. As you inhale, say to yourself, "I am relaxing my eyes and face. My eyes and face are completely relaxed." As you exhale, release all stress and tension from your eyes and face.

Focus on your head and skull. As you inhale, say to yourself, "I am relaxing my head and skull. My head and skull are completely relaxed." As you exhale, release all stress and tension from your head and skull.

You are now deeply relaxed. Every part of your body is deeply relaxed. Your mind is also deeply relaxed. Allow yourself to fully savor this state of deep relaxation. Just breathe deeply. With each inhalation, your chest and stomach are expanding. With each exhalation, your chest and stomach are contracting. Continue breathing deeply. Feel yourself fully inhabiting your body.

When you are ready, slowly move your fingers and toes. Rub your palms together and gently place them on your eyelids. Slowly open your eyes while still retaining that sense of deep restfulness in your body and mind.

GUIDED JOURNALING EXERCISES

The goal of these exercises is to help you develop self-aware-ness. As I have said many times, emotional regulation requires intense self-awareness. You must regularly get in touch with yourself to fully appreciate and experience your emotional life. All emotions are to be felt, acknowledged, and embraced. You don't have to become fixated on them or mull over them but be willing to hear what they are trying to communicate with you.

You can copy these questions in another journal and use them regularly to get in touch with yourself. You can pick just a few of these questions to answer regularly or you can use all of them. You can do the exercises every day or once in a while. It is all up to you and what works best for you.

THE PRACTICE

What is the predominant emotion you are feeling right now?

Where in your body do you feel this emotion most intensely?

What is the message that this emotion is trying to convey to you? What can you learn about your life from the experience of this emotion? Is it telling you that you are moving in the right direction or is it signaling you to make some changes?

If you feel you must make some changes to your life, then list down exactly what those changes should be.

_____

_____

_____

_____

Is there any emotion you are avoiding right now?

_____

_____

_____

_____

Why are you avoiding this emotion?

_____

_____

_____

_____

Give yourself just five minutes to fully feel this emotion that you are avoiding. You can time an alarm clock for five minutes if you wish. Tell yourself that you have to feel this emotion only for five minutes, after that you can go back to avoiding it if you wish. Now, feel this emotion fully – really try listening to this emotion. What is this emotion trying to convey to you and why is it so painful for you to hear what it has to tell you?

If you feel you must make some changes to your life based on what this emotion is conveying to you, then list down exactly what those changes should be.

CONCLUSION

I want to thank you for placing your trust in me and taking this journey together. I really hope this book has added tremendous value to your life. I would urge you to not treat it as a one-time read but keep coming back to it regularly. Emotional regulation is a skill that is built over time with consistent practice. Reading a book provides you with knowledge but skill is built only with practice. The more frequently you use the tools, techniques, methods, and ideas I have shared in this book, the more resilient you'll become.

May this be a new beginning for you! Always keep in mind that the quality of your inner world determines and influences the quality of your outer reality. You cannot change anything outside without first working on your inner world. We create the circumstances of our life based on the type of person we have been so far along the way. To live a different kind of life, we have to transform ourselves into the type of person who is truly capable of living our ideal lifestyle.

Life is about learning and growing. The more you learn, the more skills you build – the more you grow. With perpetual growth, you are guaranteed to keep upgrading and leveling up your life. Who you want to be and how you want to live your life is in your own hands. No matter what kind of cards you have been dealt with, you can get the best out of yourself and out of life. It is all about adopting and practicing the right attitude.

When life strikes you down, don't allow yourself to writhe in self-pity. Allow yourself to feel the pain and shed a few tears, then focus all your energy on getting back up. No matter what happens, you can always come back stronger and better. The wheels of destiny are compelled to favor those who constantly seek more and refuse to settle for anything less than what they truly desire. While you are going after your dreams, be sure to keep yourself centered and grounded by practicing the emotional regulation techniques, tools, and methods you have learned. Love yourself and take care of yourself. You are worthy of it!

Self-love and self-care should be a way of life for all of us. We can create a beautiful life for ourselves and for our loved ones, only when we truly love ourselves. If you are looking for more practical tools and techniques, then you may want to check out my *I am Capable of Anything* series which has unique daily affirmations for each day of the year. If self-love is an area of real struggle for you, then you may also want to check out my *Radical Self-Love* book.

Sincerely,

S.S. Leigh

REFERENCES

Attachment Theory. Wikipedia. (n.d.). Retrieved January 28, 2023, from https://en.wikipedia.org/wiki/Attachment_theory

Bergland, C. (2015, May 9). *How Do Your Genes Influence Levels of Emotional Sensitivity?* Psychology Today. Retrieved January 28, 2023, from https://www.psychologytoday.com/us/blog/the-athletes-way/201505/how-do-your-genes-influence-levels-emotional-sensitivity

Card, O. S. (n.d.). **Quoted in** Goodreads. Retrieved January 28, 2023, from https://www.goodreads.com/quotes/19828-this-is-how-humans-are-we-question-all-our-beliefs

Chopra, D. (n.d.). **Quoted in** BrainyQuote. Retrieved January 28, 2023, from https://www.brainyquote.com/quotes/deepak_chopra_453950

Cloud, H. (n.d.). *Quoted in* Goodreads. Retrieved January 28, 2023, from https://www.goodreads.com/quotes/790608-boundaries-define-us-they-define-what-is-me-and-what

DeLoach, N. (n.d.). *Quoted in* AZ Quotes. Retrieved January 28, 2023, from https://www.azquotes.com/quote/1511617

Dweck, C. S. (2007). *Mindset: The New Psychology of Success.* Ballantine Books.

Guendelman, S., Medeiros, S., & Rampes, H. (2017, March 6). *Mindfulness and emotion regulation: Insights from neurobiological, psychological, and clinical studies.* Frontiers. Retrieved January 28, 2023, from https://www.frontiersin.org/articles/10.3389/fpsyg.2017.00220/full

Holt, M. E., Lee, J. W., Morton, K. R., & Tonstad, S. (2014). *Mediterranean diet and Emotion Regulation.* NCBI. Retrieved January 28, 2023, from https://www.ncbi.nlm.nih.gov/pmc/articles/PMC6350904/

Kiyosaki, R. T. (n.d.). *Quoted in* Goodreads. Retrieved January 28, 2023, from https://www.goodreads.com/quotes/1185231-learn-to-use-your-emotions-to-think-not-think-with

Mayer, J. D. (n.d.). *Quoted in* Quotefancy. Retrieved January 28, 2023, from https://quotefancy.com/quote/1714976

Mayo Clinic Staff. (2022, August 3). *Exercise and stress: Get moving to manage stress.* Mayo Clinic. Retrieved January 28, 2023, from https://www.mayoclinic.org/healthy-lifestyle/stress-management/in-depth/exercise-and-stress/art-20044469

McEwen, B. S. (2003, August). *Early Life Influences on Life-Long Patterns of Behavior and Health.* PubMed. Retrieved January 28, 2023, from https://pubmed.ncbi.nlm.nih.gov/12953293/

Nagda, H. (n.d.). *Quoted in* Goodreads. Retrieved January 28, 2023, from https://www.goodreads.com/author/quotes/21178772

Nicolai, E. (n.d.). *Quoted in* Goodreads. Retrieved January 28, 2023, from https://www.goodreads.com/author/quotes/7303179.ELLE_NICOLAI

Robbins, M. (2017). *The 5 Second Rule: Transform Your Life, Work, and Confidence with Everyday Courage.* Mel Robbins Productions Inc.

Rohn, J. (n.d.). *Quoted in* Goodreads. Retrieved January 28, 2023, from https://www.goodreads.com/quotes/1798-you-are-the-average-of-the-five-people-you-spend

Socrates. (n.d.). *Quoted in* BrainyQuote. Retrieved January 28, 2023, from https://www.brainyquote.com/quotes/socrates_101168

Sogunle, K. (n.d.). *Quoted in* Goodreads. Retrieved January 28, 2023, from https://www.goodreads.com/work/quotes/53979331-beyond-the-pain-by-kemi-sogunle

Stone, W. C. (n.d.). *Quoted in* BrainyQuote. Retrieved January 28, 2023, from https://www.brainyquote.com/quotes/w_clement_stone_193778

Tahir, S. (n.d.). *Quoted in* Goodreads. Retrieved January 28, 2023, from https://www.goodreads.com/quotes/7778144-your-emotions-make-you-human-even-the-unpleasant-ones-have

Thought. Wikipedia. (n.d.). Retrieved January 28, 2023, from https://en.wikipedia.org/wiki/Thought

University of Tokyo. (2021, March 19). *Study shows stronger brain activity after writing on paper than on tablet or smartphone*. ScienceDaily. Retrieved January 28, 2023, from https://www.sciencedaily.com/releases/2021/03/210319080820.htm

What is Behavior? NSW Health. (n.d.). Retrieved January 28, 2023, from https://www.health.nsw.gov.au/mental-health/psychosocial/principles/Pages/behaviour-whatis.aspx

Williams, A. (n.d.). *Quoted in* 60 Law of Attraction Quotes to Boost Your Willpower. Quote Ambition. Retrieved January 28, 2023, from https://www.quoteambition.com/law-of-attraction-quotes/